Maths Practice Reception

Question Book

Sarah-Anne Fernandes

Name ______________________________

Schofield&Sims

Introduction

The **Schofield & Sims Maths Practice Reception Question Book** uses step-by-step practice to develop children's understanding of key early mathematical concepts.

The structure

This book focuses on ensuring secure knowledge of the numbers 1 to 20 in line with the Early Years Foundation Stage Early Learning Goals. There is a particular emphasis on the numbers 1 to 10. Children address each numeral with a set of questions dedicated to learning to write, count and recognise the number.

In addition to its focus on number, this book offers children the opportunity to extend their skills to ensure they are confident as they progress into Year 1. Early calculation is introduced through simple, age-appropriate questions. Children can improve their position, shape and measure skills, look for patterns and make connections. They also see maths used in topics connected to everyday life, such as coins and time, which encourages development of a positive attitude towards maths.

At the back of the book, there is a 'Final practice' section. Here, mixed questions are used to check children's understanding of the knowledge and skills acquired throughout the book and identify any areas that need to be revisited.

A mastery approach

The **Primary Practice Maths** series follows a knowledge-based mastery approach. Children deepen their learning by applying and representing their knowledge and skills in multiple ways. This approach reinforces number concepts, nurtures fluency and strengthens both reasoning and problem-solving skills. Integral to this approach is the use of visual representations of mathematical concepts. Some of the most common visual representations used in this book are:

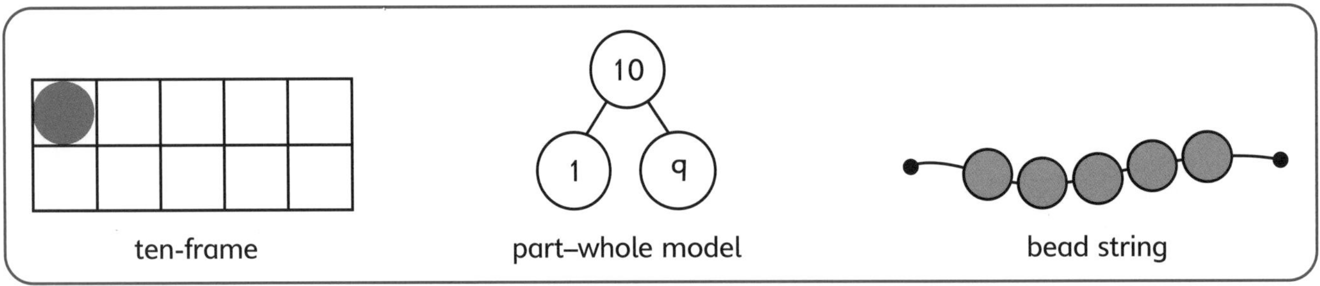

ten-frame part–whole model bead string

Writing numbers

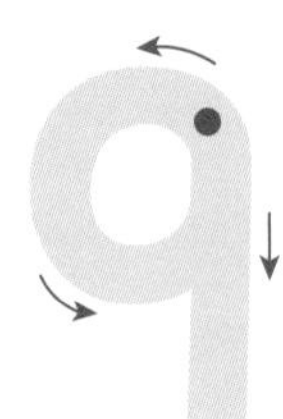

The number units provide children with the opportunity to develop their handwriting skills for the digits 0 to 9. Children practise by tracing numbers to ensure they form numbers smoothly. Tracing patterns include a dot to indicate where letter formation begins. Children then progress to copying numbers independently and finally to answering problems involving the numbers they have practised.

Online answers

Answers for every question in this book are available to download from the **Schofield & Sims** website. The answers are accompanied by detailed explanations where helpful. There is also a progress chart, allowing children to track their learning as they complete each set of questions, and an editable certificate.

Contents

The number 1

Remember

1

one

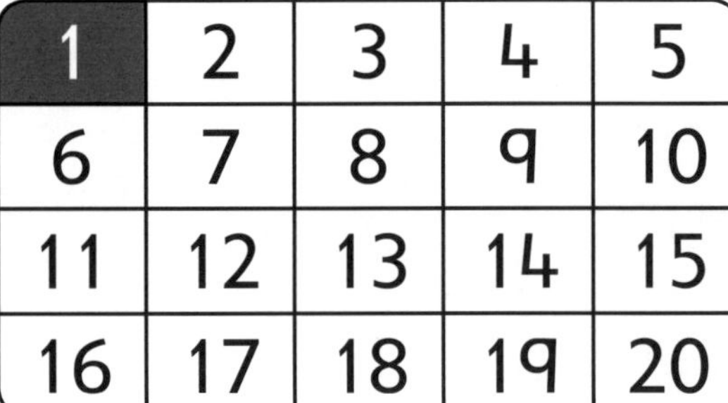

1	2	3	4	5
6	7	8	9	10
11	12	13	14	15
16	17	18	19	20

1. **Trace** the number 1.

2. **Copy** the number 1.

3. **Colour** 1 cherry on top of the cake.

4 **Write** in the box how many cars you can see.

5 **Circle** the picture that does **not** show 1.

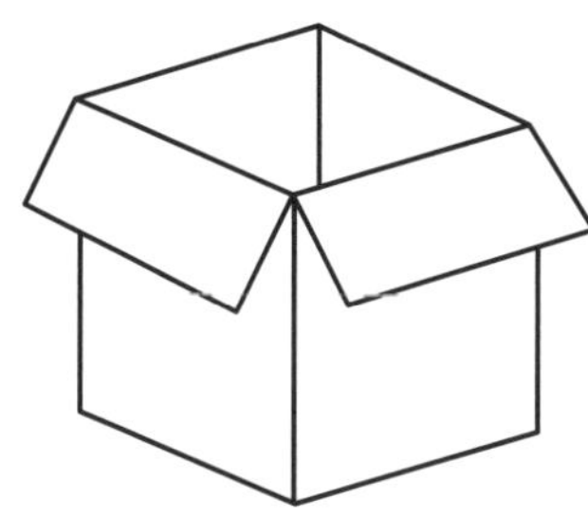

6 **Draw** 1 counter on the ten-frame.

The number 2

Remember

2

two

1	2	3	4	5
6	7	8	9	10
11	12	13	14	15
16	17	18	19	20

1. **Trace** the number 2.

2 2 2 2 2 2

2. **Copy** the number 2.

_____ _____ _____ _____ _____ _____

3. **Draw** 2 wings on the butterfly.

4) **Write** in the box how many cartons of orange juice you can see.

5) **Circle** the picture that does **not** show 2.

6) **Draw** 2 counters on the ten-frame.

The number 3

Remember

3

three

1	2	3	4	5
6	7	8	9	10
11	12	13	14	15
16	17	18	19	20

1. **Trace** the number 3.

3 3 3 3 3 3

2. **Copy** the number 3.

_____ _____ _____ _____ _____ _____

3. **Colour** 3 cars.

4) **Write** in the box how many books you can see.

5) **Circle** the picture that does **not** show 3.

6) **Draw** 3 counters on the ten-frame.

The number 4

Remember

4

four

1	2	3	**4**	5
6	7	8	9	10
11	12	13	14	15
16	17	18	19	20

1. **Trace** the number 4.

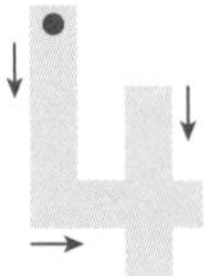     

2. **Copy** the number 4.

_____ _____ _____ _____ _____ _____

3. **Colour** the 4 seasons.

winter

spring

summer

autumn

4 **Write** in the box how many flowers you can see.

5 **Circle** the picture that does **not** show 4.

6 **Draw** 4 counters on the ten-frame.

The number 5

Remember

5

five

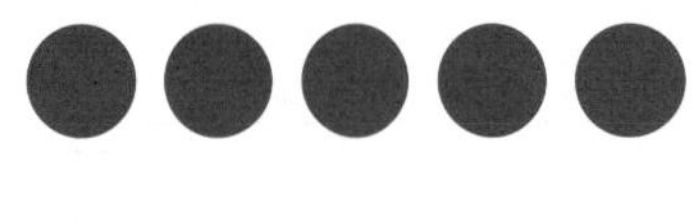

1	2	3	4	5
6	7	8	9	10
11	12	13	14	15
16	17	18	19	20

① **Trace** the number 5.

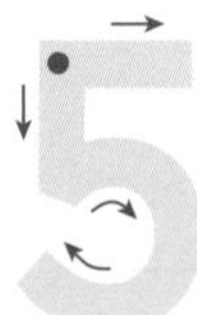

5 5 5 5 5 5

② **Copy** the number 5.

_____ _____ _____ _____ _____ _____

③ **Colour** 5 bananas.

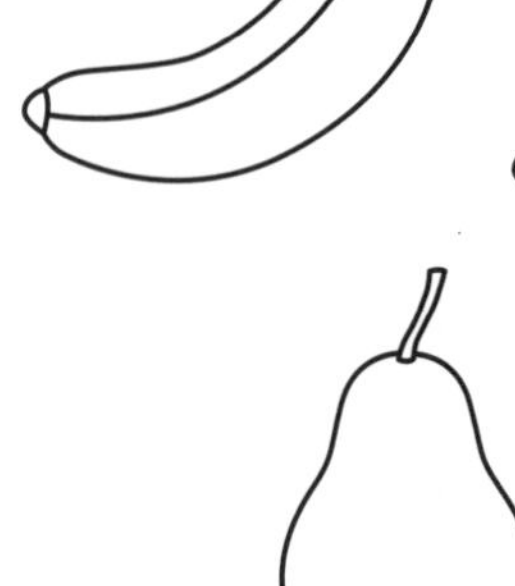
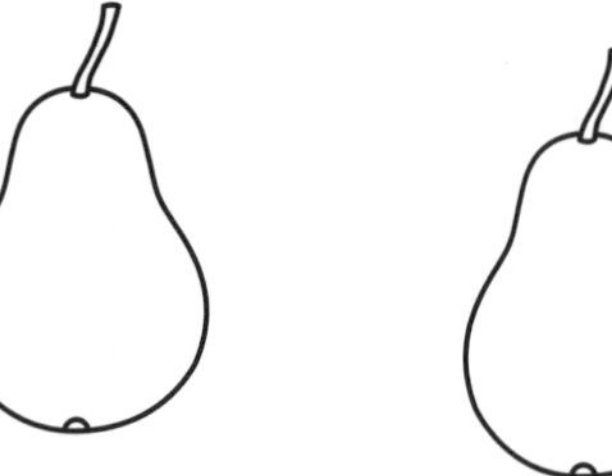
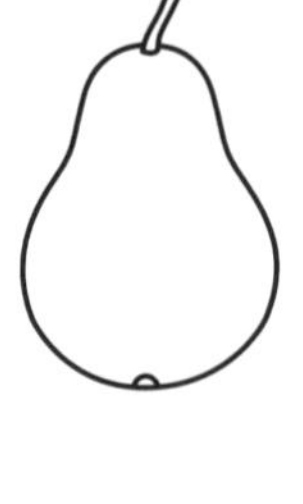
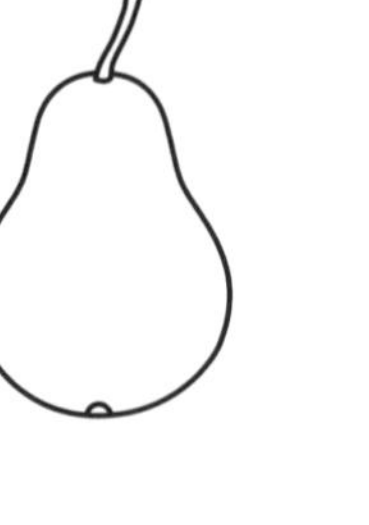

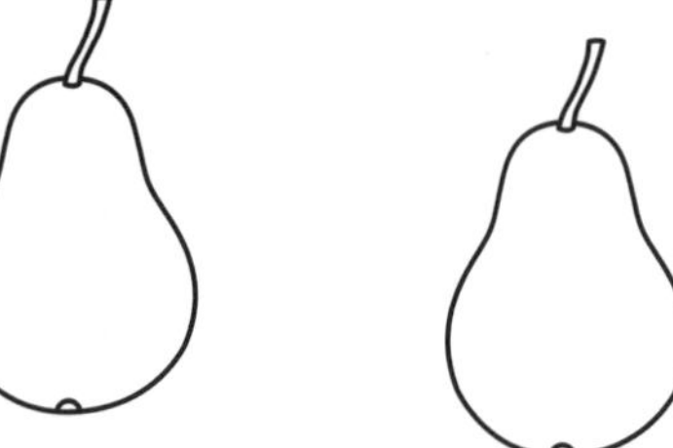

4. **Write** in the box how many cans of drink you can see.

5. **Circle** the picture that does **not** show 5.

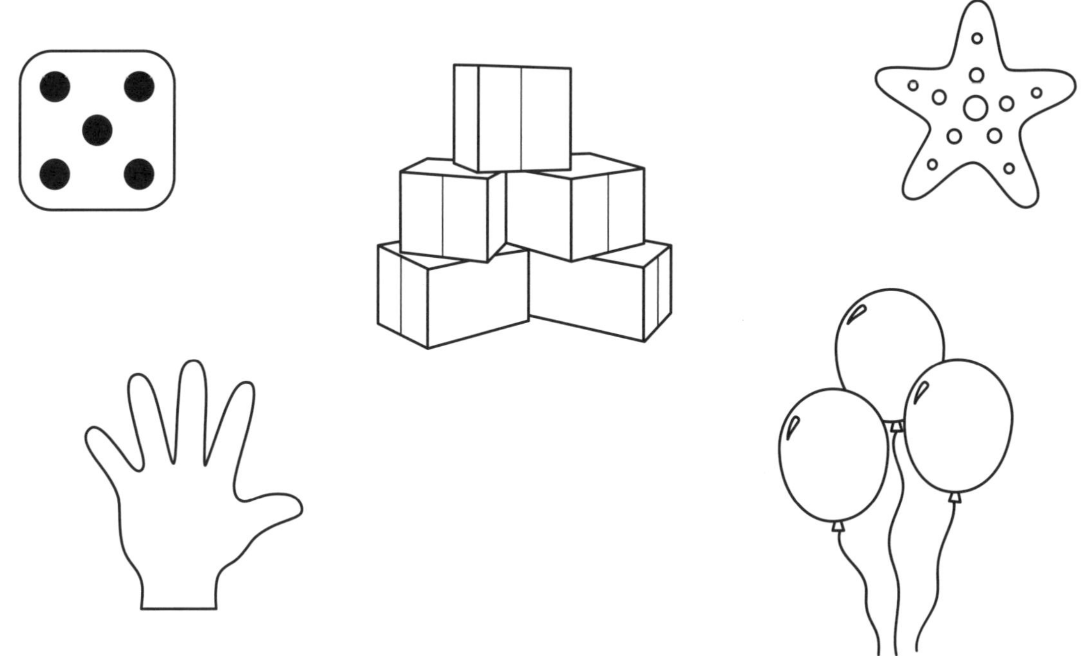

6. **Draw** 5 counters on the ten-frame.

Counting to 5

1) **Count** the number of apples in each bag. **Write** the numbers in the boxes.

2) **Draw** 3 balloons in the box.

3) **Fill in** the missing numbers on the train.

4) **Count** the number of cakes on each plate. **Tick** the plate with the most cakes.

5) **Count** the number of blocks in each tower. **Tick** the tower with the fewest blocks.

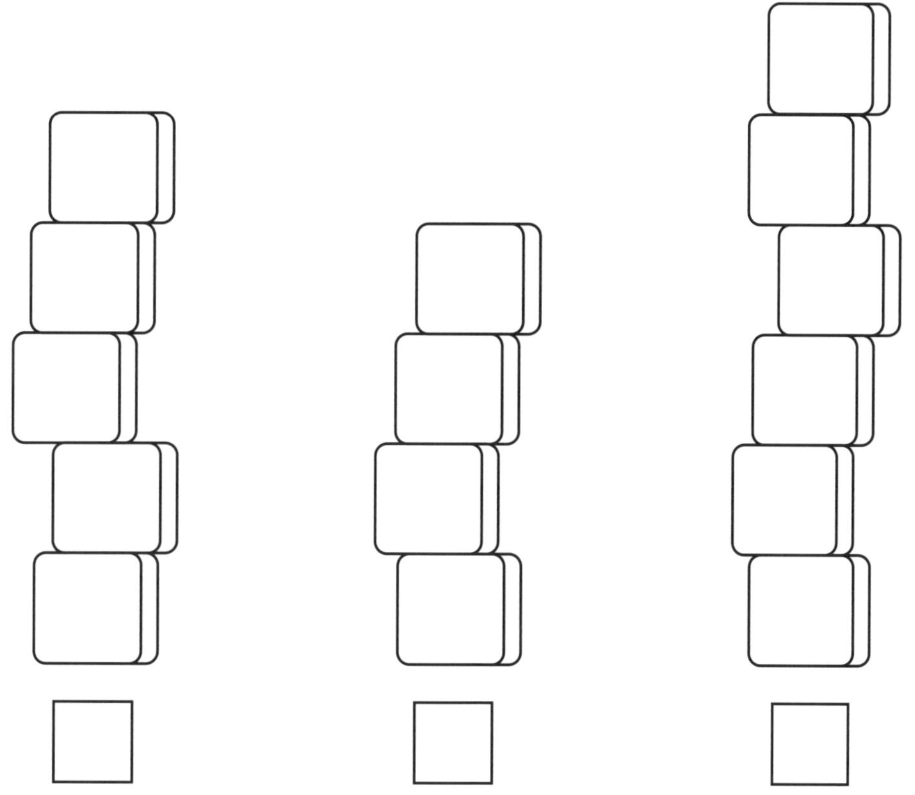

6) **Circle** the dice that have fewer than 5 dots.

Number facts to 5

1 **Write** the number of stars in each box to make the number statement to 5.

and makes 5 ☐ + ☐ = 5

2 **Fill in** the missing numbers to make the bottom two numbers add up to the top number. Use the blocks to help.

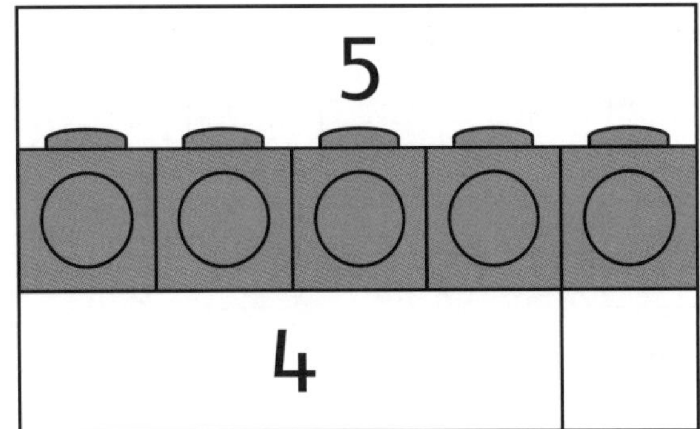

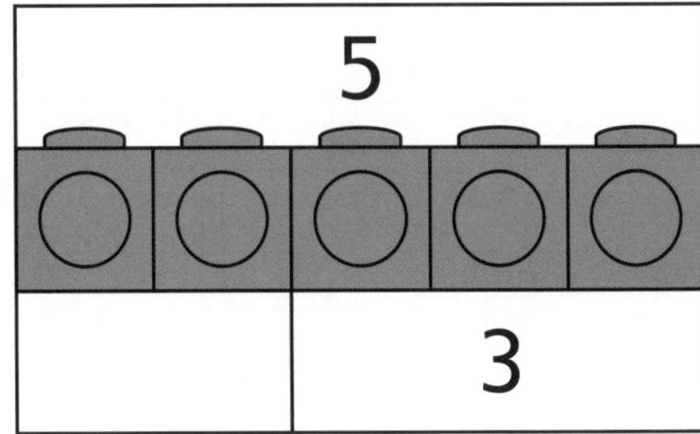

3 **Draw** dots on the dice to make 5.

☐ + ☐ = 5 ☐ + ☐ = 5

4 **Fill in** the missing numbers in the part–whole models.
The bottom two numbers add up to the top number.
One has been done for you.

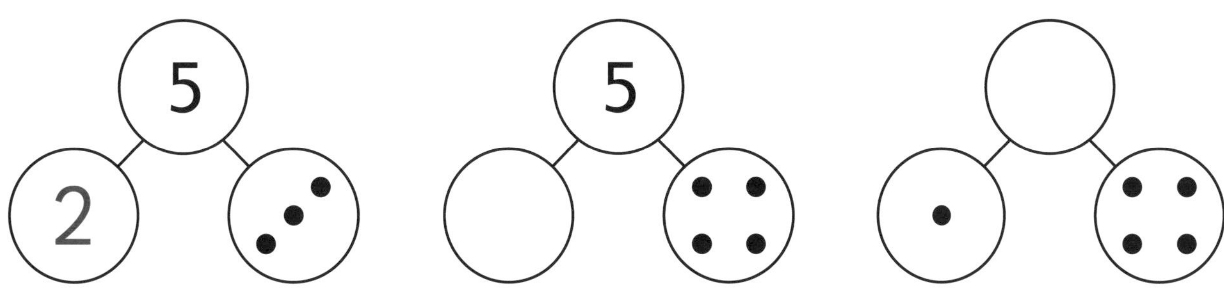

5 **Solve** the number stories. **Write** the answers in the boxes.

Taj has 3 cars. Mia has 2 cars. How many cars do they have together?

There are 4 oranges and 1 apple in the bowl. How many pieces of fruit are there in total?

The number 6

Remember

6

six

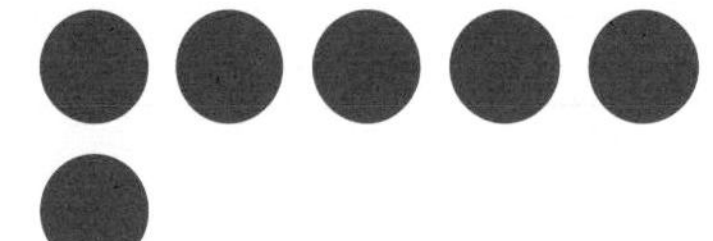

1	2	3	4	5
6	7	8	9	10
11	12	13	14	15
16	17	18	19	20

① **Trace** the number 6.

② **Copy** the number 6.

______ ______ ______ ______ ______ ______

③ **Draw** more spots so that each ladybird has 6 spots.

4 **Write** in the box how many bees you can see.

5 **Circle** the picture that does **not** show 6.

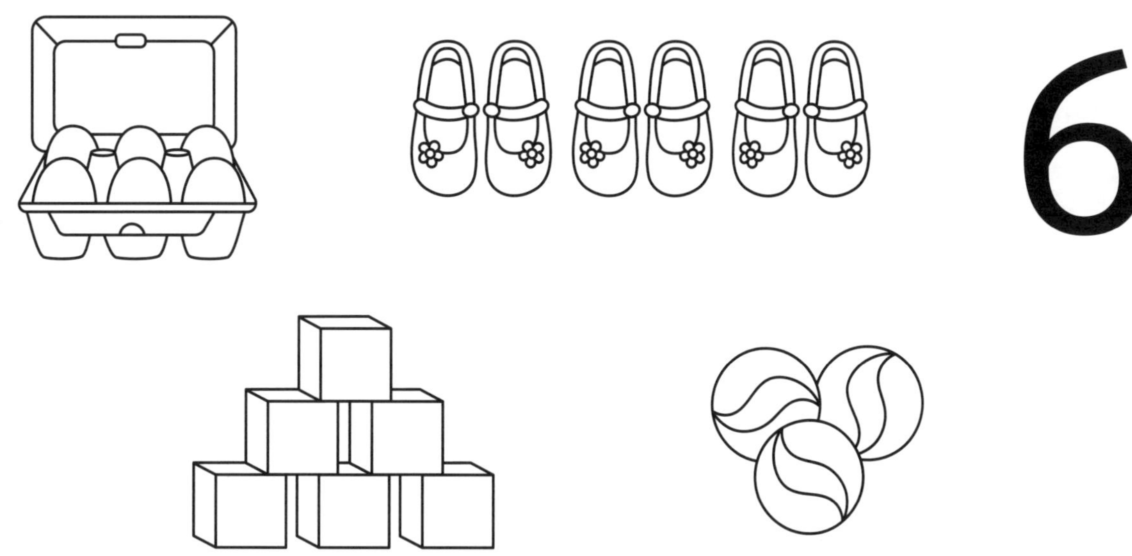

6 **Draw** 6 counters on the ten-frame.

The number 7

Remember

7

seven

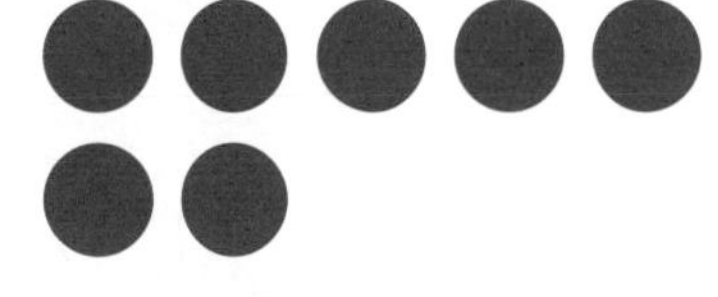

1	2	3	4	5
6	7	8	9	10
11	12	13	14	15
16	17	18	19	20

1. **Trace** the number 7.

7 7 7 7 7 7

2. **Copy** the number 7.

______ ______ ______ ______ ______ ______

3. **Colour** the 7 colours on the rainbow.

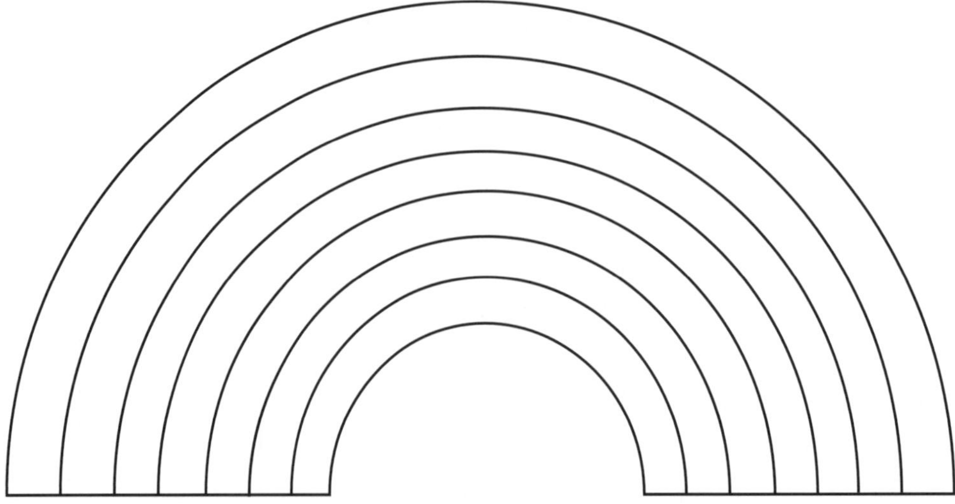

4) **Write** in the box how many mice you can see.

5) **Circle** the picture that does **not** show 7.

6) **Draw** 7 counters on the ten-frame.

The number 8

Remember

8

eight

1	2	3	4	5
6	7	**8**	9	10
11	12	13	14	15
16	17	18	19	20

1. **Trace** the number 8.

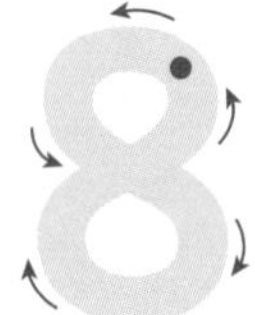     

2. **Copy** the number 8.

_____ _____ _____ _____ _____ _____

3. **Colour** 8 shells.

4 **Write** in the box how many spotty party hats you can see.

5 **Circle** the picture that does **not** show 8.

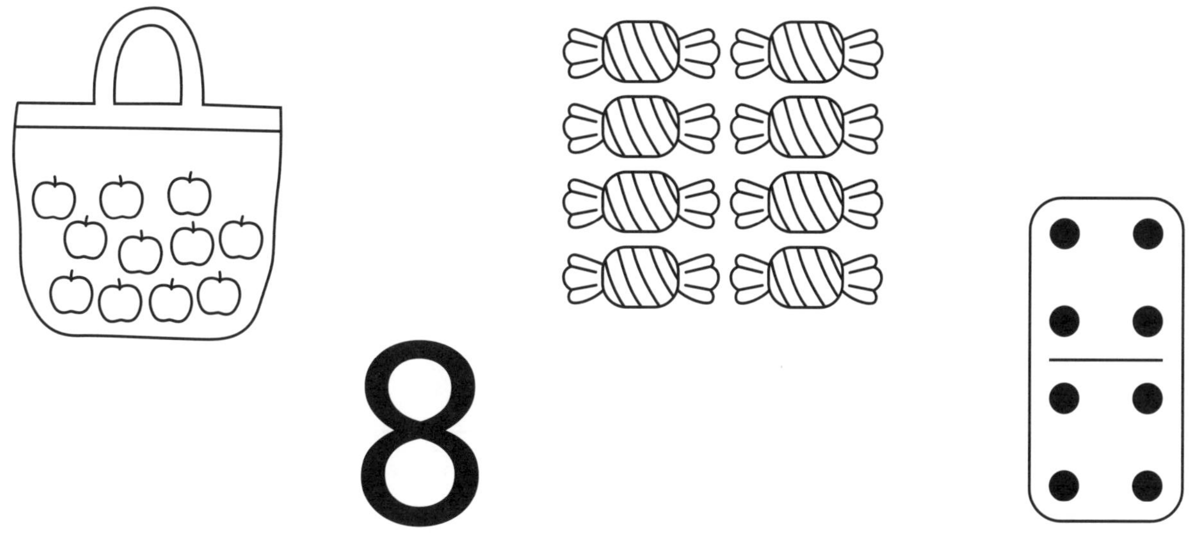

6 **Draw** 8 counters on the ten-frame.

The number 9

Remember

9

nine

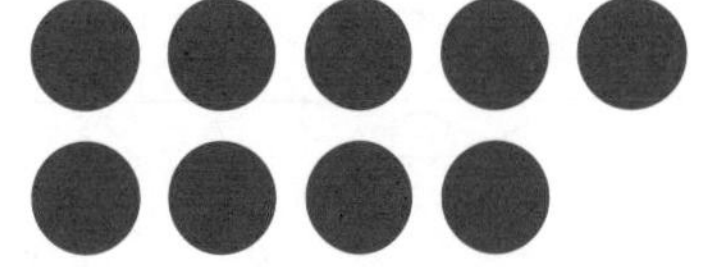

1	2	3	4	5
6	7	8	9	10
11	12	13	14	15
16	17	18	19	20

1. **Trace** the number 9.

9 9 9 9 9 9

2. **Copy** the number 9.

______ ______ ______ ______ ______ ______

3. **Colour** 9 pencils.

4 **Write** in the box how many doughnuts you can see.

5 **Circle** the picture that does **not** show 9.

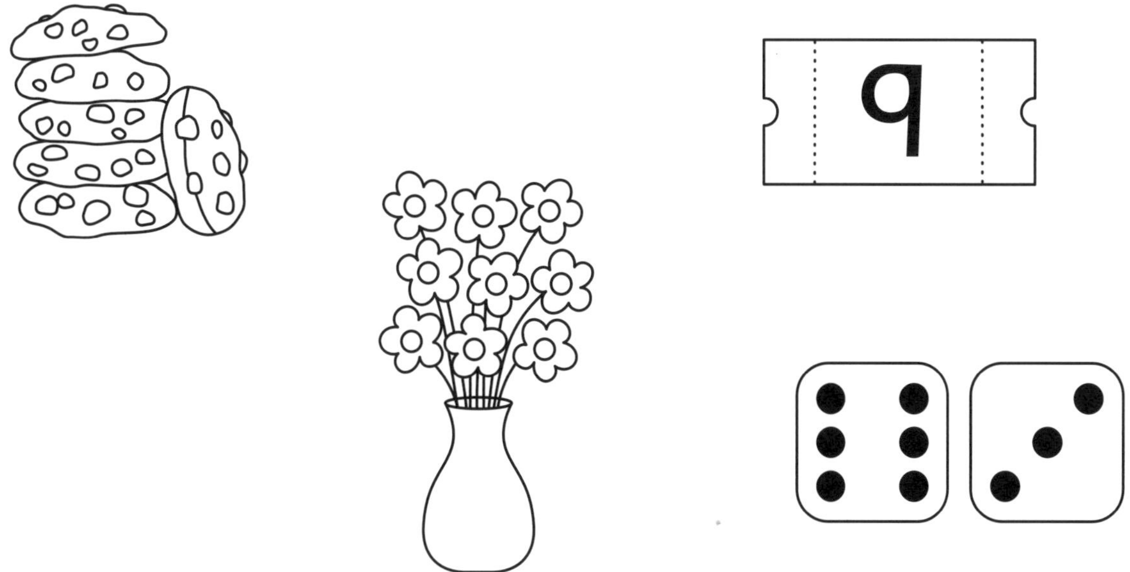

6 **Draw** 9 counters on the ten-frame.

The number 10

Remember

10

ten

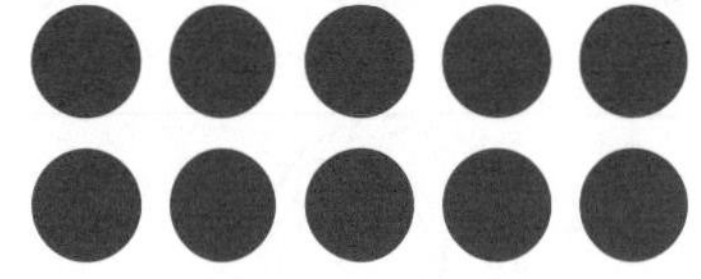

1	2	3	4	5
6	7	8	9	10
11	12	13	14	15
16	17	18	19	20

1. **Trace** the number 10.

10 10 10 10 10

2. **Copy** the number 10.

3. **Colour** 10 stars.

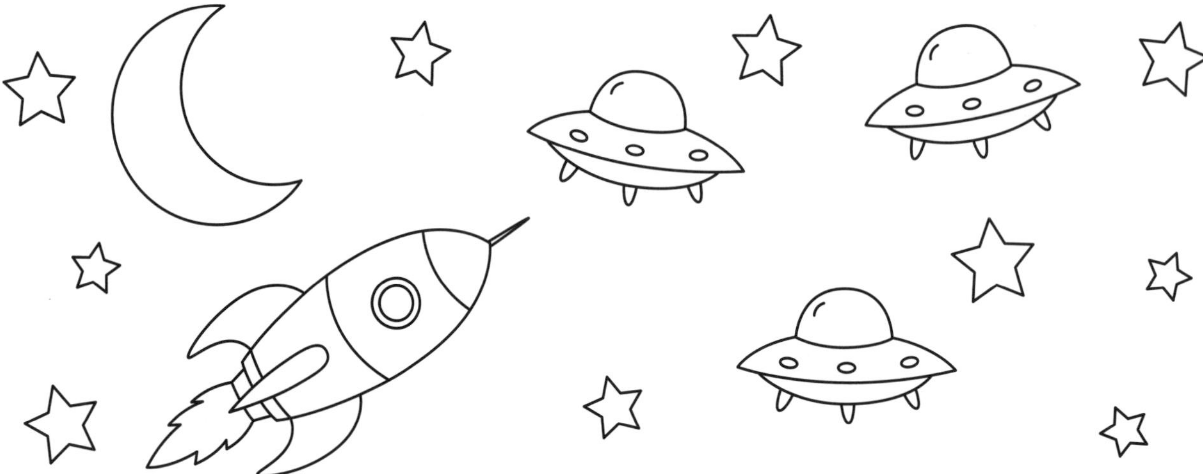

4. **Write** in the box how many spoons you can see.

5. **Circle** the picture that does **not** show 10.

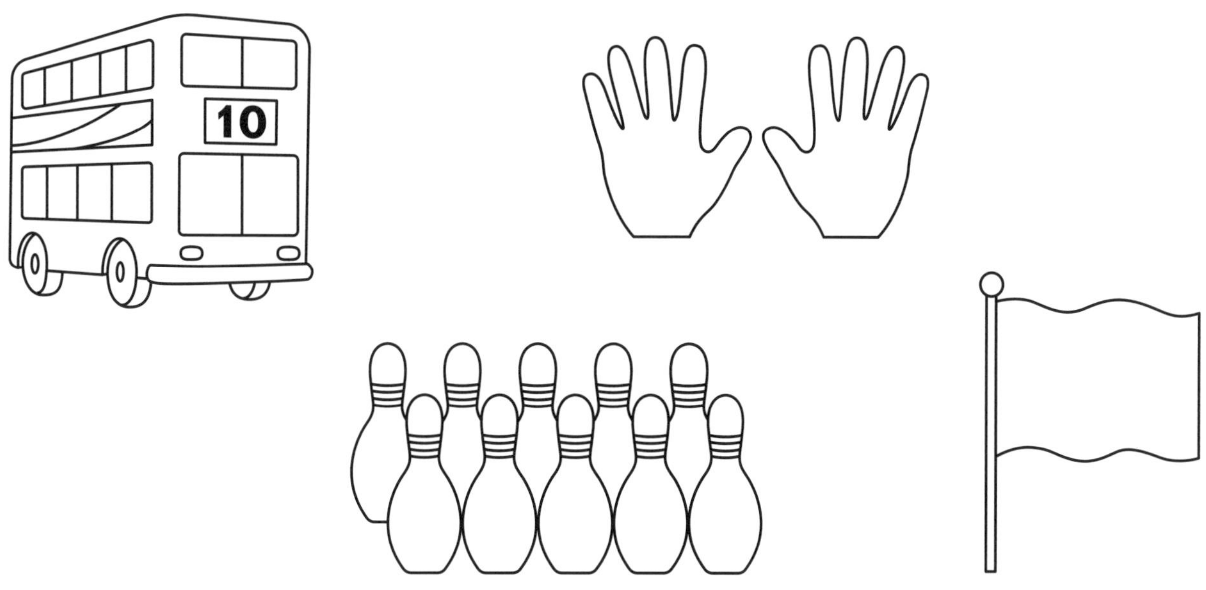

6. **Draw** 10 counters on the ten-frame.

Counting to 10

1 **Draw lines** to match each set of pictures with the correct number.

5

3

7

2. **Fill in** the missing numbers to launch the rocket.

1			4	
			9	

3. **Draw** the correct number of counters on each ten-frame.

4 counters

6 counters

3 counters

8 counters

4. **Count** the number of eggs in each box. **Tick** the box with the most eggs.

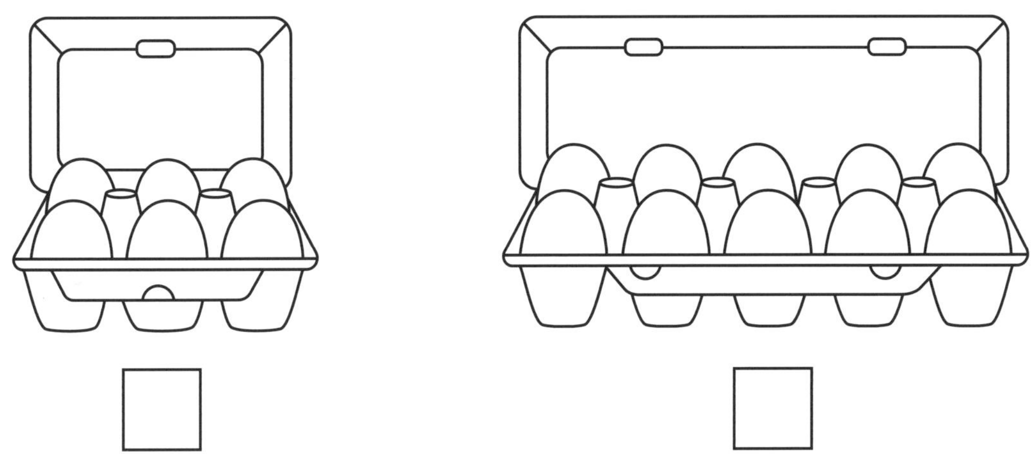

Number facts to 10

1. **Write** in each box the number of red beads and white beads to make a number statement that adds to 10. One has been done for you.

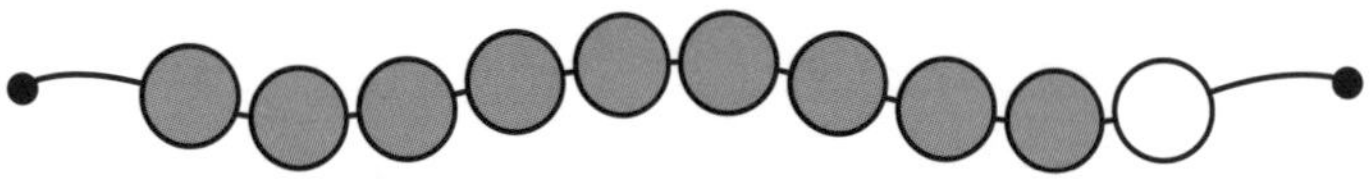

9 + 1 = 10

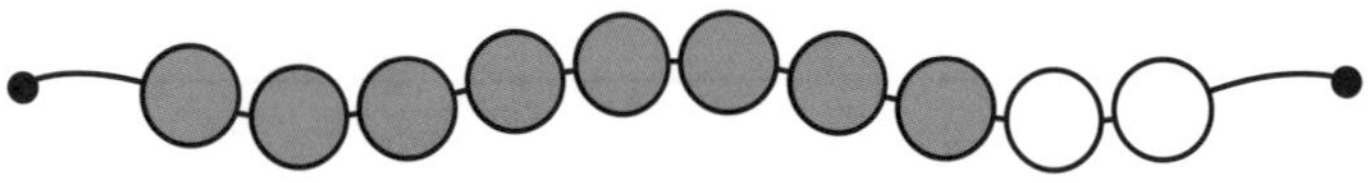

☐ + ☐ = 10

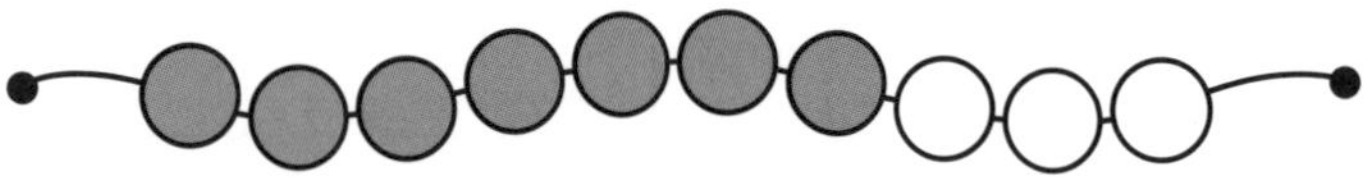

☐ + ☐ = 10

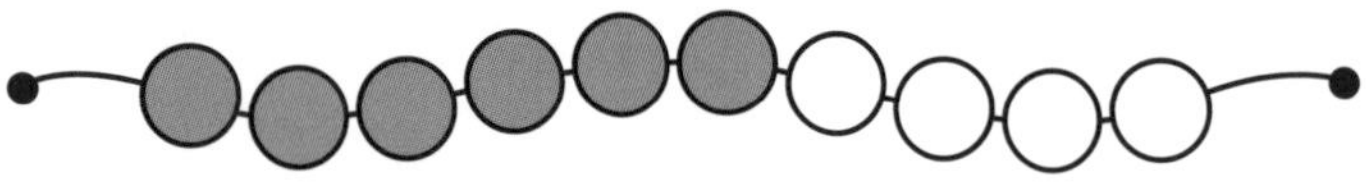

☐ + ☐ = 10

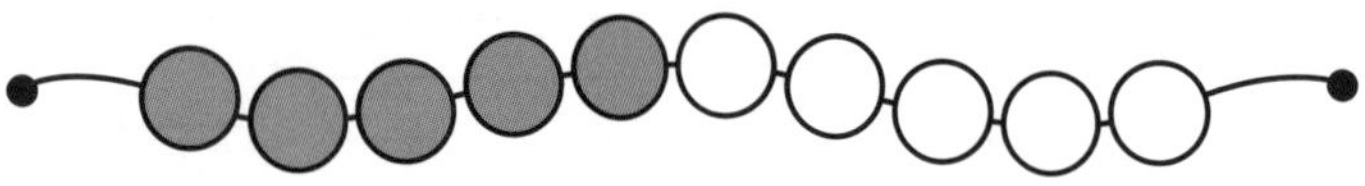

☐ + ☐ = 10

2 **Fill in** the missing numbers in the bar models. The two bottom numbers add up to the top number.

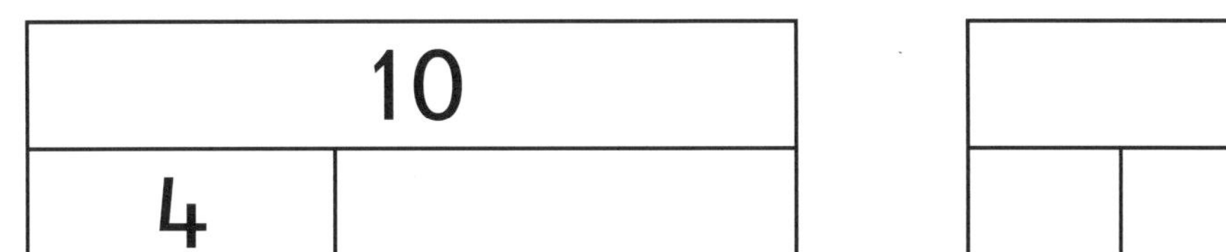

10	
4	

10	
	8

3 **Fill in** the missing numbers in the part–whole models. The two bottom numbers add up to the top number.

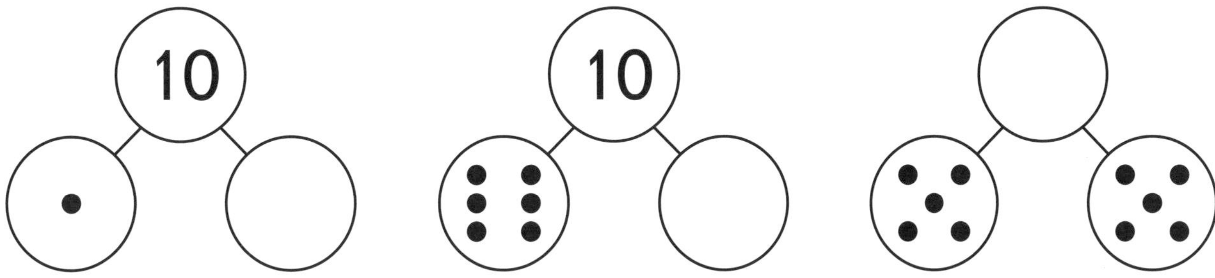

4 **Solve** the number stories. **Write** the answers in the boxes.

Ben has 3 pencils. Kim has 7 pencils. How many pencils do they have together?

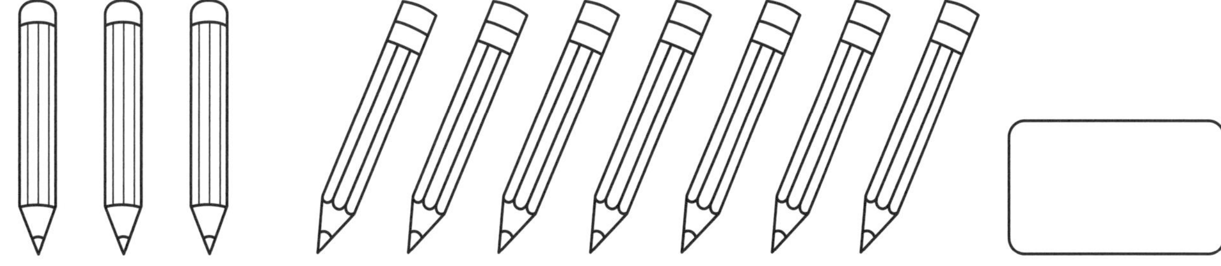

There are 8 plain doughnuts and 2 doughnuts with sprinkles. How many doughnuts are there in total?

The number 11

Remember

11

eleven

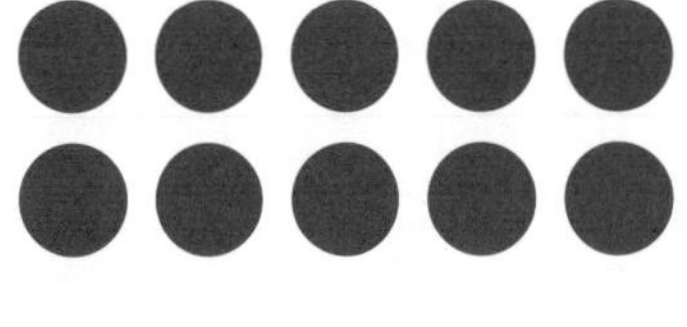

1	2	3	4	5
6	7	8	9	10
11	12	13	14	15
16	17	18	19	20

1. **Trace** the number 11.

11 11 11 11 11

2. **Copy** the number 11.

________ ________ ________ ________

3. **Circle** 11 marbles.

The number 12

Remember

12
twelve

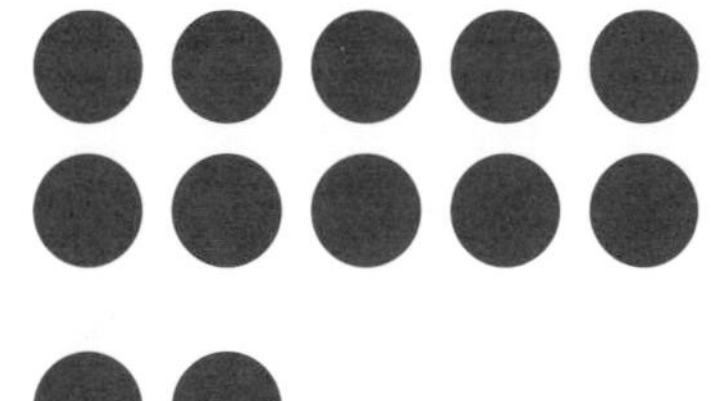

1	2	3	4	5
6	7	8	9	10
11	12	13	14	15
16	17	18	19	20

1. **Trace** the number 12.

12 12 12 12 12

2. **Copy** the number 12.

3. **Colour** 12 eggs in the box.

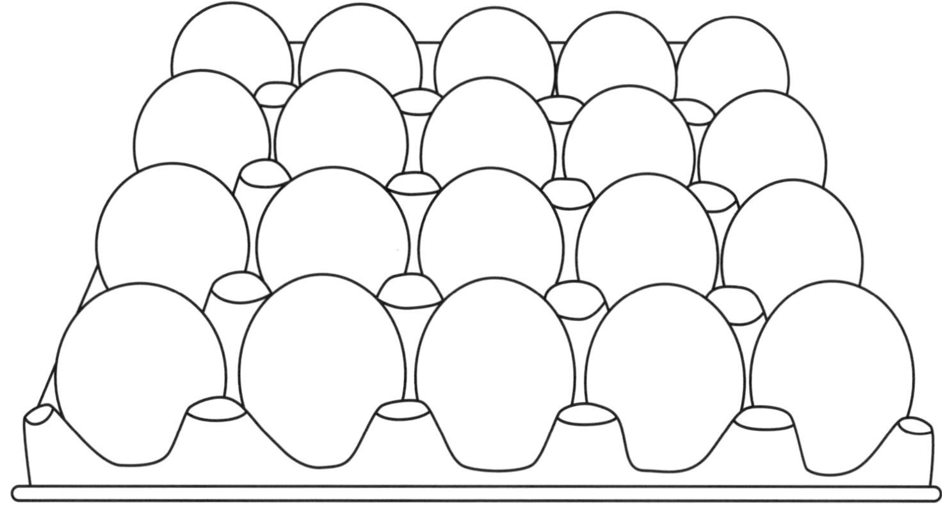

The number 13

Remember

13

thirteen

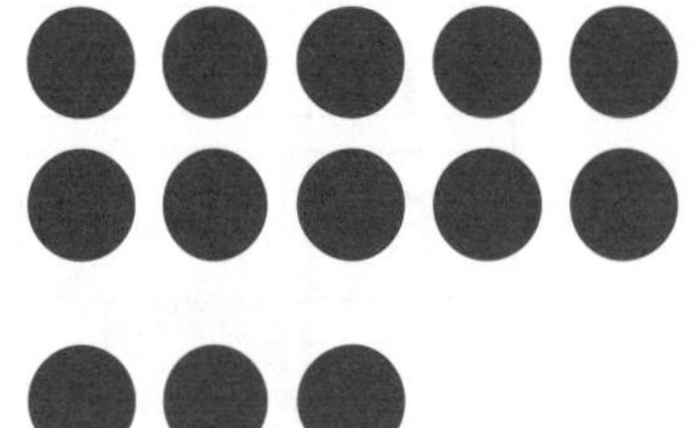

1	2	3	4	5
6	7	8	9	10
11	12	13	14	15
16	17	18	19	20

1. **Trace** the number 13.

13 13 13 13 13

2. **Copy** the number 13.

________ ________ ________ ________

3. **Cross out** 13 stars.

The number 14

Remember

14

fourteen

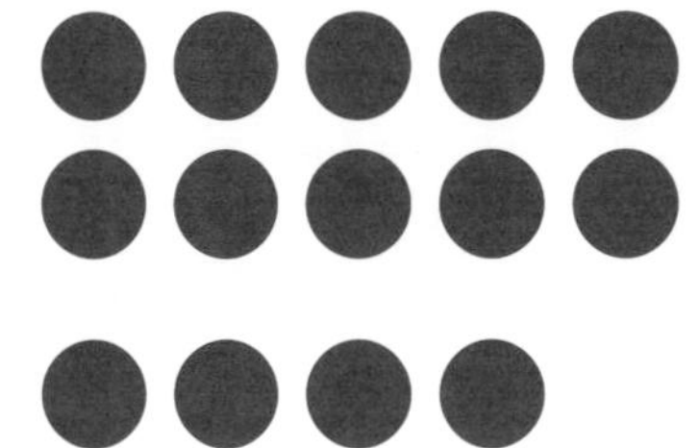

1	2	3	4	5
6	7	8	9	10
11	12	13	14	15
16	17	18	19	20

1. **Trace** the number 14.

2. **Copy** the number 14.

3. **Count** the number of large, round buttons you can see. **Write** the number in the box.

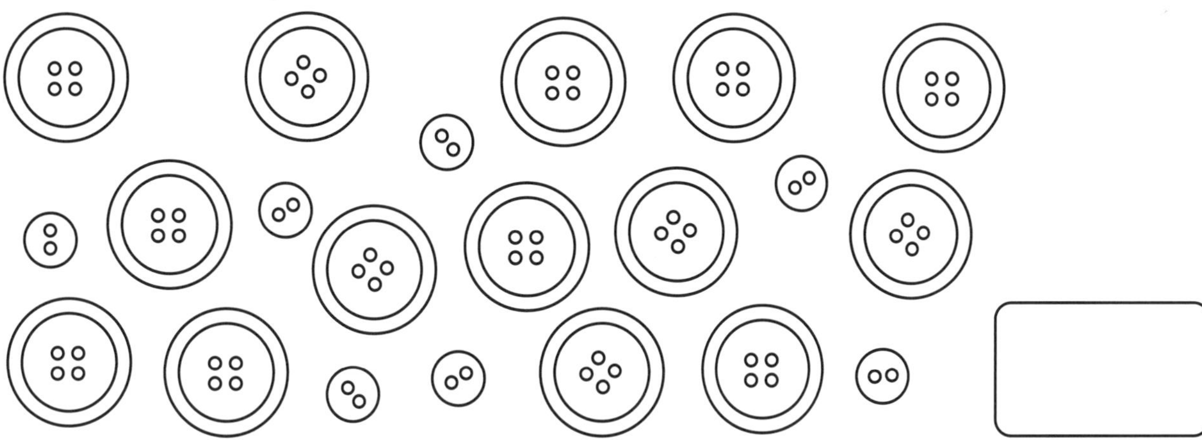

The number 15

Remember

15

fifteen

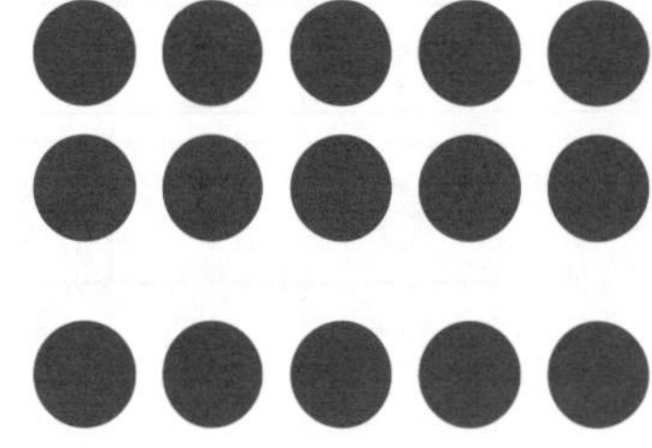

1	2	3	4	5
6	7	8	9	10
11	12	13	14	**15**
16	17	18	19	20

① **Trace** the number 15.

15 15 15 15 15

② **Copy** the number 15.

________ ________ ________ ________

③ **Circle** 15 cupcakes.

The number 16

Remember

16

sixteen

1	2	3	4	5
6	7	8	9	10
11	12	13	14	15
16	17	18	19	20

1. **Trace** the number 16.

16 16 16 16 16

2. **Copy** the number 16.

______ ______ ______ ______

3. **Write** in the box how many legs **two** spiders have.

The number 17

Remember

17

seventeen

1	2	3	4	5
6	7	8	9	10
11	12	13	14	15
16	17	18	19	20

1. **Trace** the number 17.

17 17 17 17 17

2. **Copy** the number 17.

________ ________ ________ ________

3. **Tick** the set that shows 17 worms.

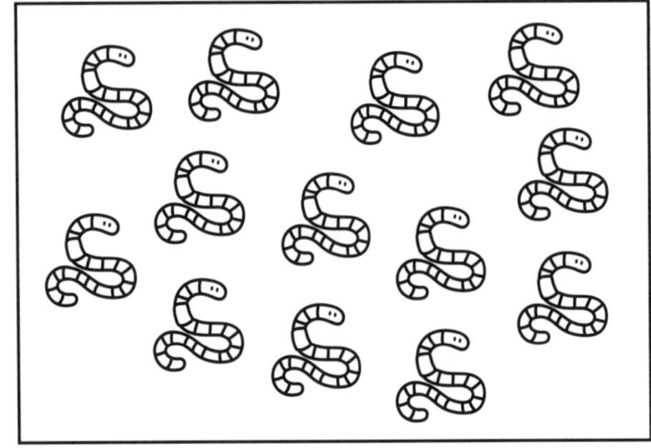

☐

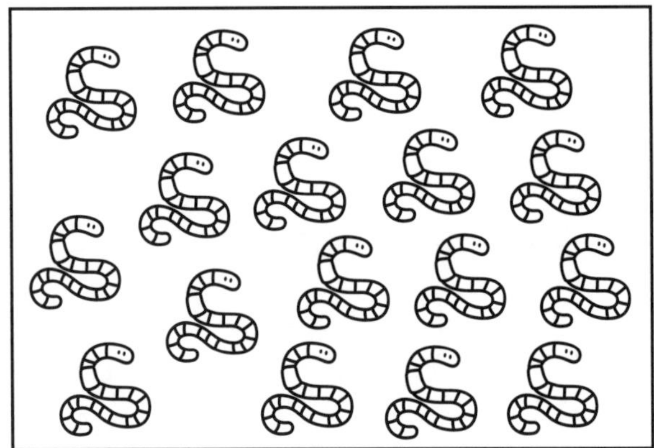

☐

The number 18

Remember

18
eighteen

1	2	3	4	5
6	7	8	9	10
11	12	13	14	15
16	17	18	19	20

1. **Trace** the number 18.

18 18 18 18 18

2. **Copy** the number 18.

3. **Draw** 18 candles on the cake.

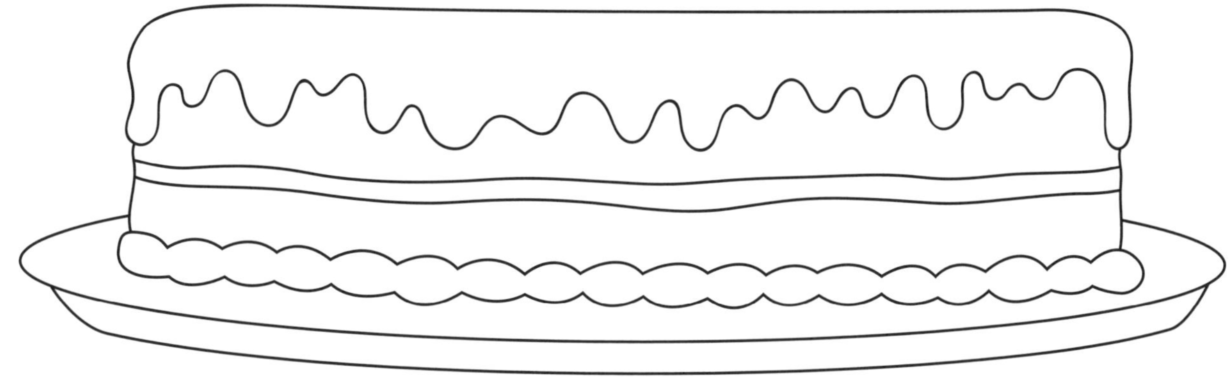

The number 19

Remember

19

nineteen

1	2	3	4	5
6	7	8	9	10
11	12	13	14	15
16	17	18	19	20

1. **Trace** the number 19.

19 19 19 19 19

2. **Copy** the number 19.

________ ________ ________ ________

3. **Write** in the box how many fish you can see.

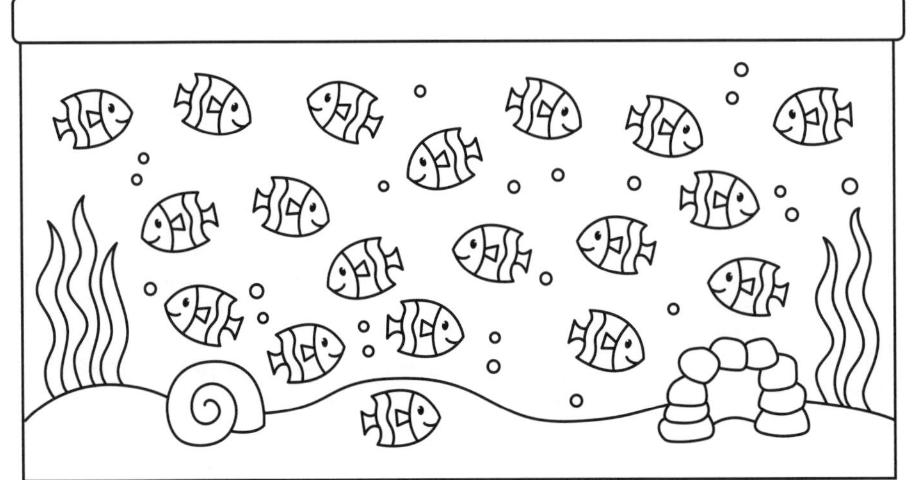

The number 20

Remember

20

twenty

1	2	3	4	5
6	7	8	9	10
11	12	13	14	15
16	17	18	19	20

1. **Trace** the number 20.

20 20 20 20 20

2. **Copy** the number 20.

__________ __________ __________ __________

3. **Draw** 10 juggling balls for each clown.

Counting to 20

1 **Count** the objects in the picture. **Write** the numbers in the boxes.

There are ☐ presents. 

There are  cupcakes. 

There are  party hats. 

2 **Draw** 20 counters on the ten-frames.

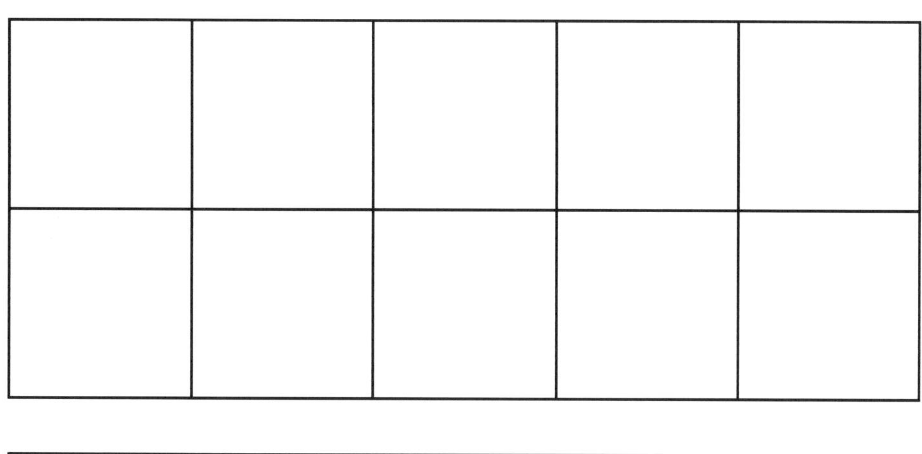

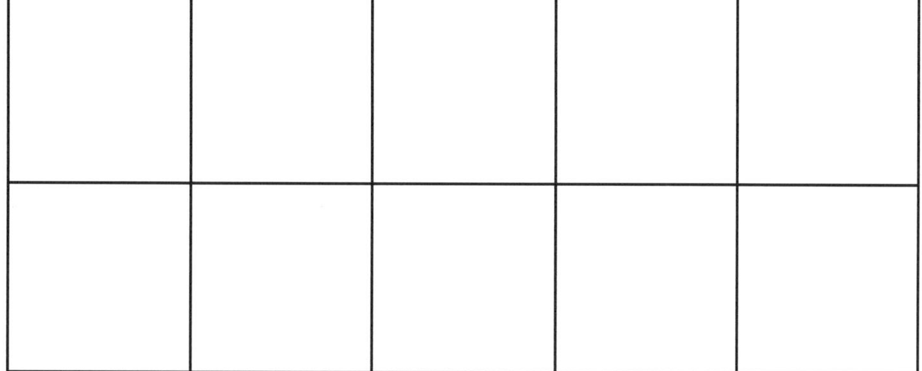

3 **Join the dots** to make a picture.

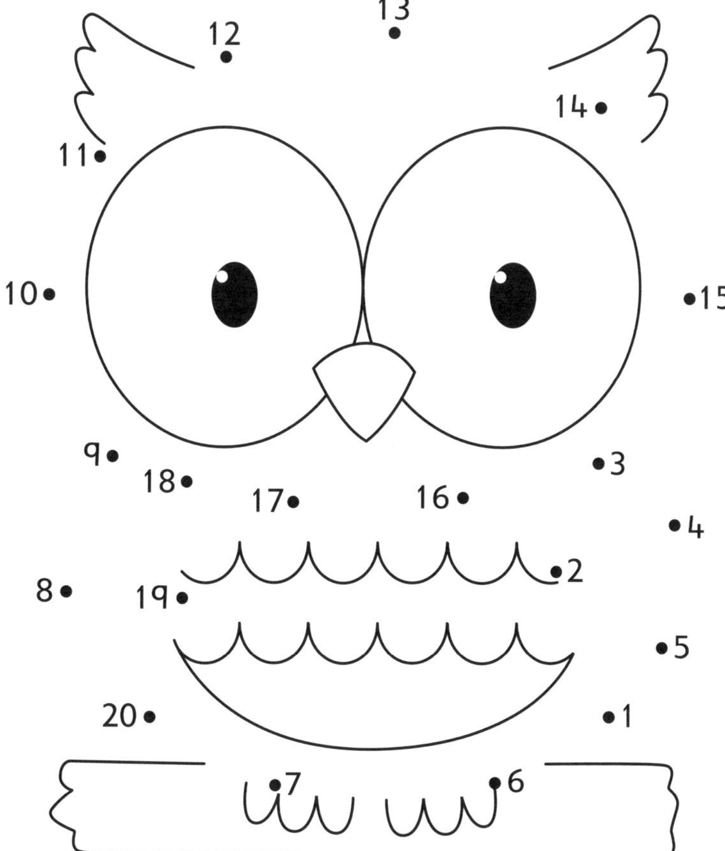

Number patterns (odd and even)

1. **Count** the number of blocks. **Write** if the number is **odd** or **even**. One has been done for you.

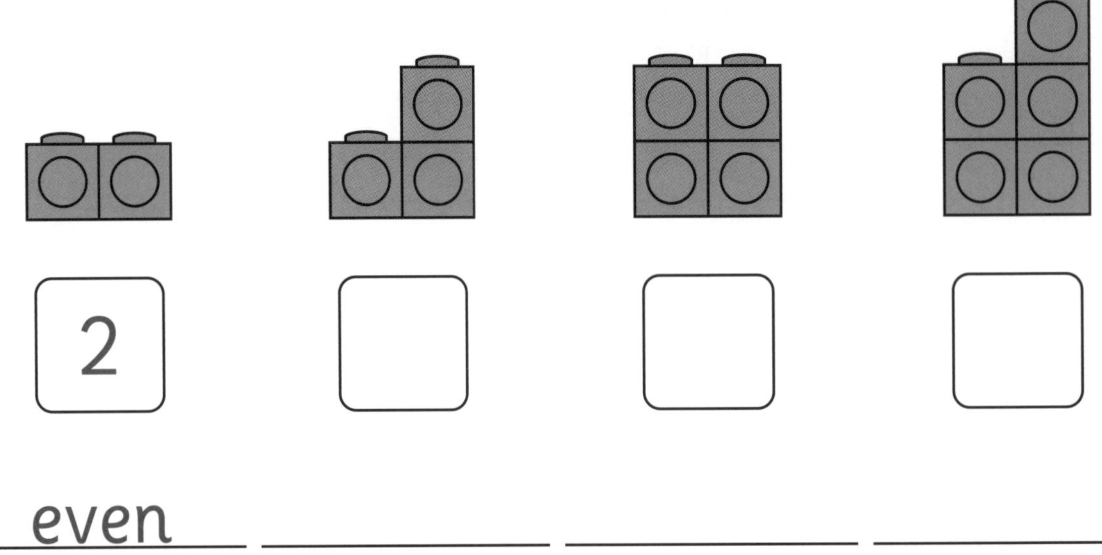

2. **Draw circles** to put the shoes into pairs. **Circle odd** or **even**. One has been done for you.

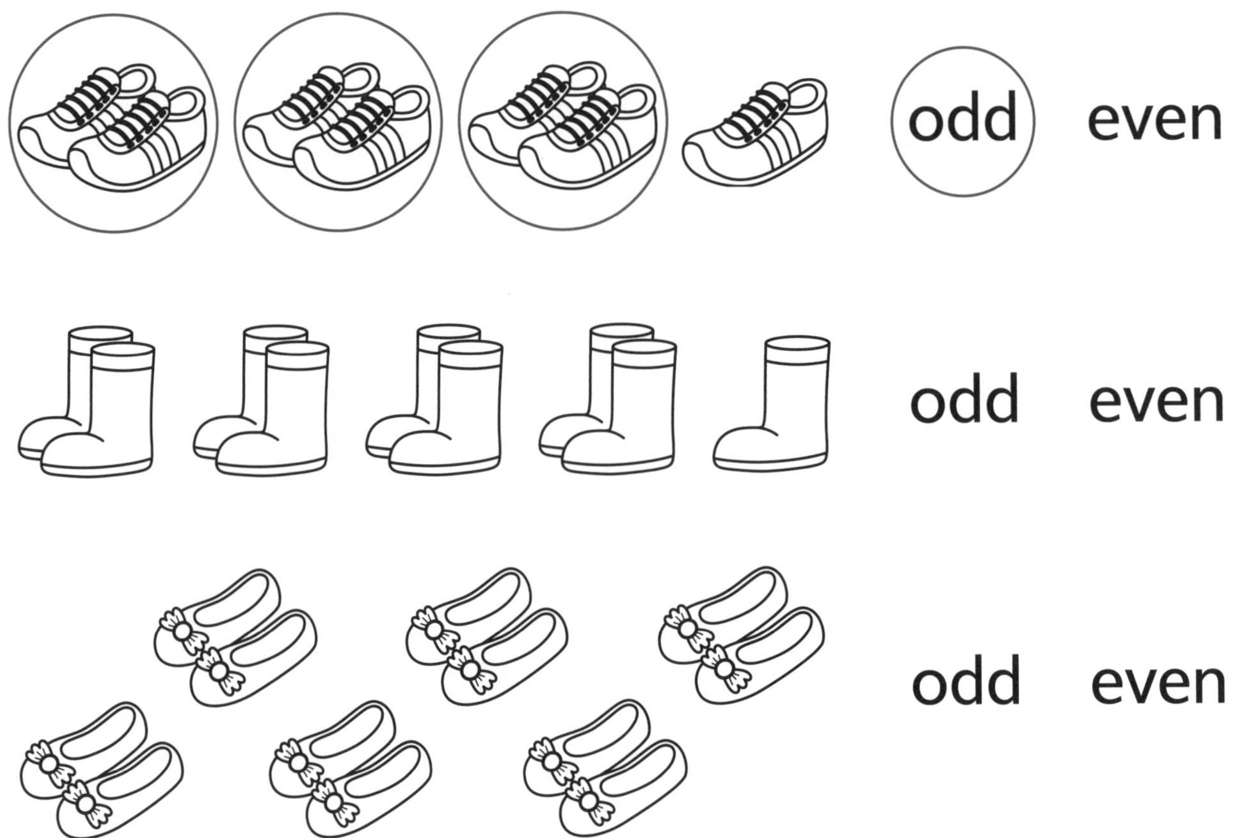

3) **Draw lines** to post each letter into the correct post box.

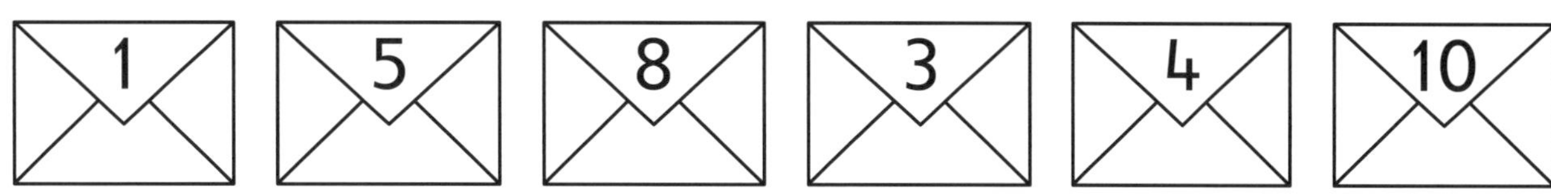

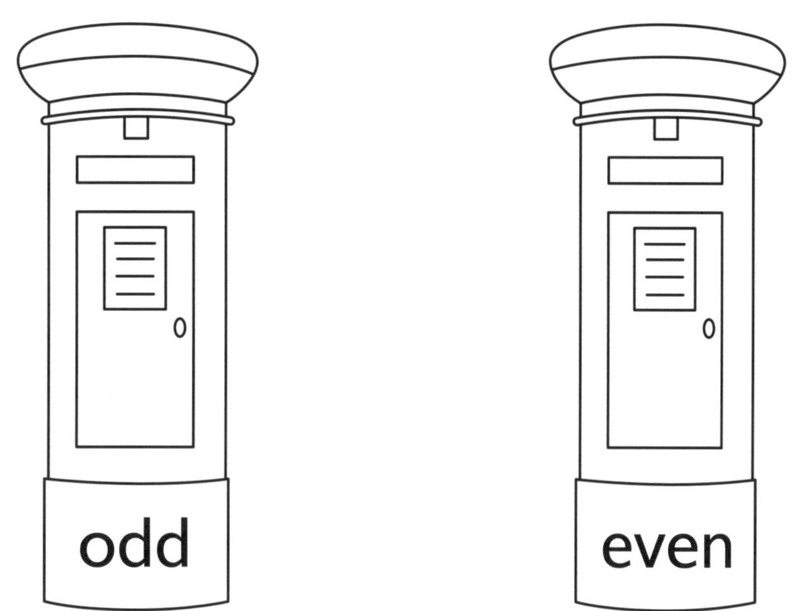

4) **Write** the **odd** numbers between 10 and 20 on these houses.

5) **Write** the **even** numbers between 11 and 20 on these houses.

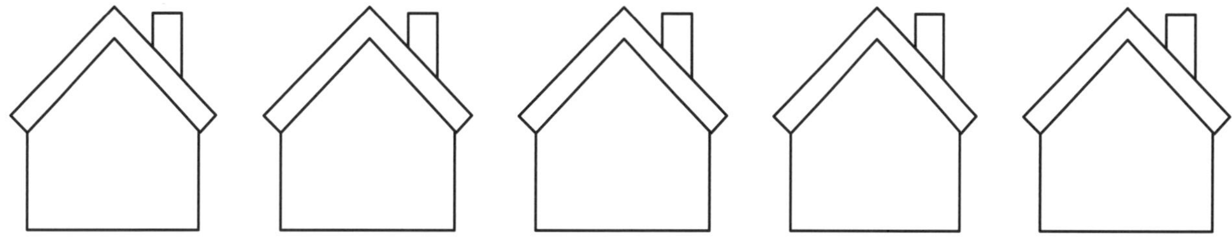

Finding 1, 2 or 3 more

① **Write** how many sweets there are altogether.

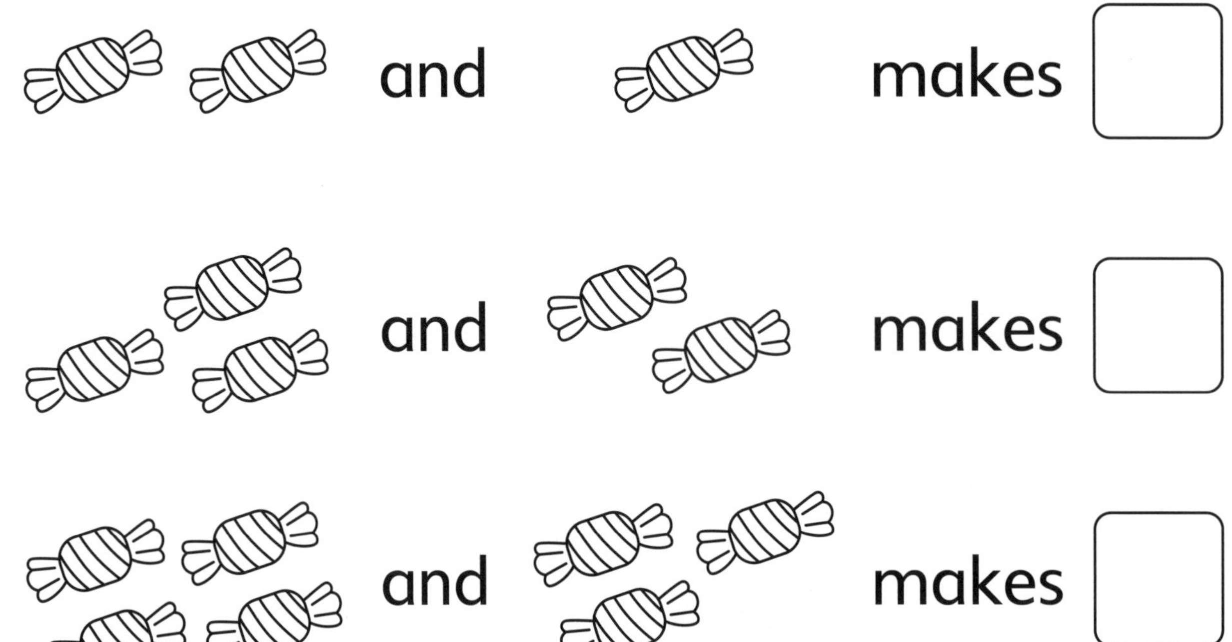

② **Write** a number statement to match the picture.

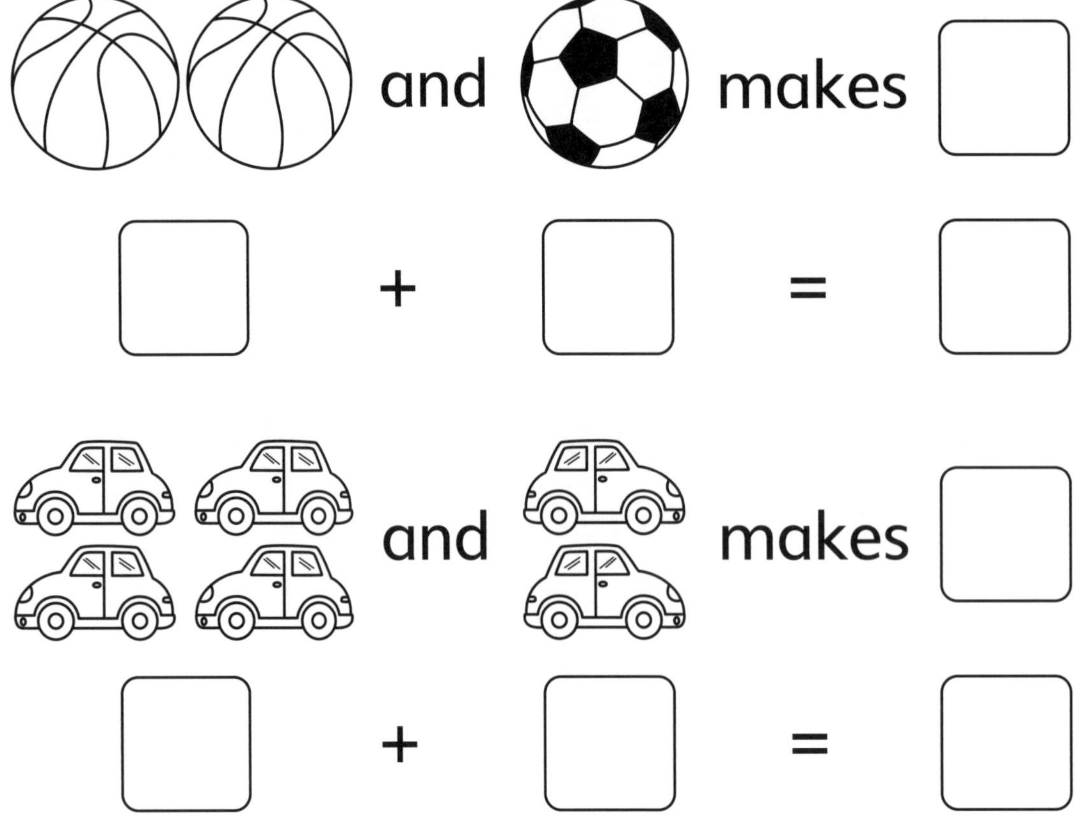

3 **Use** the number line to find the answers.

0 1 2 3 4 5 6 7 8 9 10

6 + 1 = ________ 4 + 2 = ________

2 + 3 = ________ 5 + 1 = ________

4 + 3 = ________ 8 + 2 = ________

4 **Solve** the number stories.

Jack has 2 presents. Asha has 3 presents.
How many presents do they have in total?

There are 7 shells on the beach and 2 shells in the bucket. How many shells are there altogether?

Finding 1, 2 or 3 less

1 **Write** how many are left.

Cross out 1 cupcake to find the answer.

5 − 1 = ☐

Cross out 2 apples to find the answer.

5 − 2 = ☐

Cross out 3 beans to find the answer.

  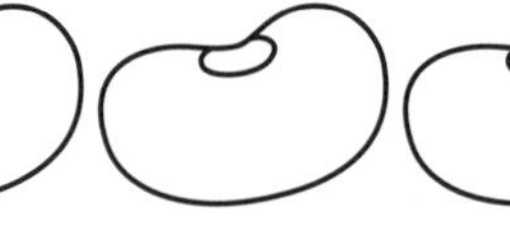

5 − 3 = ☐

2 **Write** a number statement to match the picture.

 −  = 

☐ − ☐ = ☐

3 **Use** the number line to find the answers.

0 1 2 3 4 5 6 7 8 9 10

7 − 1 = ______ 6 − 2 = ______

4 − 2 = ______ 8 − 1 = ______

5 − 3 = ______ 9 − 2 = ______

4 **Solve** the number stories.

There are 8 pencils in a pot. Ada takes 2.
How many pencils are left in the pot?

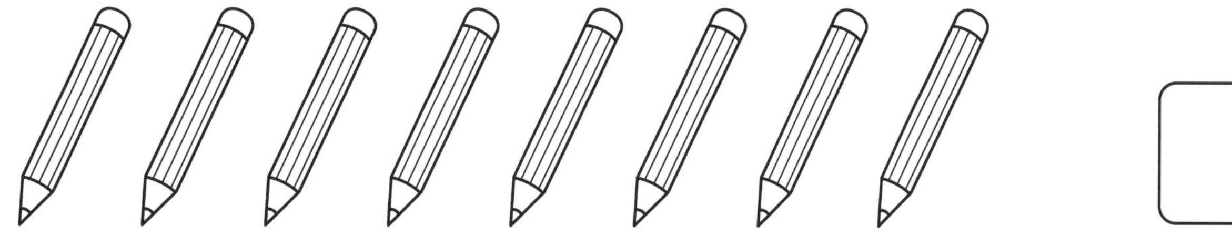

There are 7 birds on the tree. 3 birds fly away.
How many birds are left?

Doubling

1 **Draw** the same number of spots on the other side of each ladybird. How many spots does each ladybird have in total?

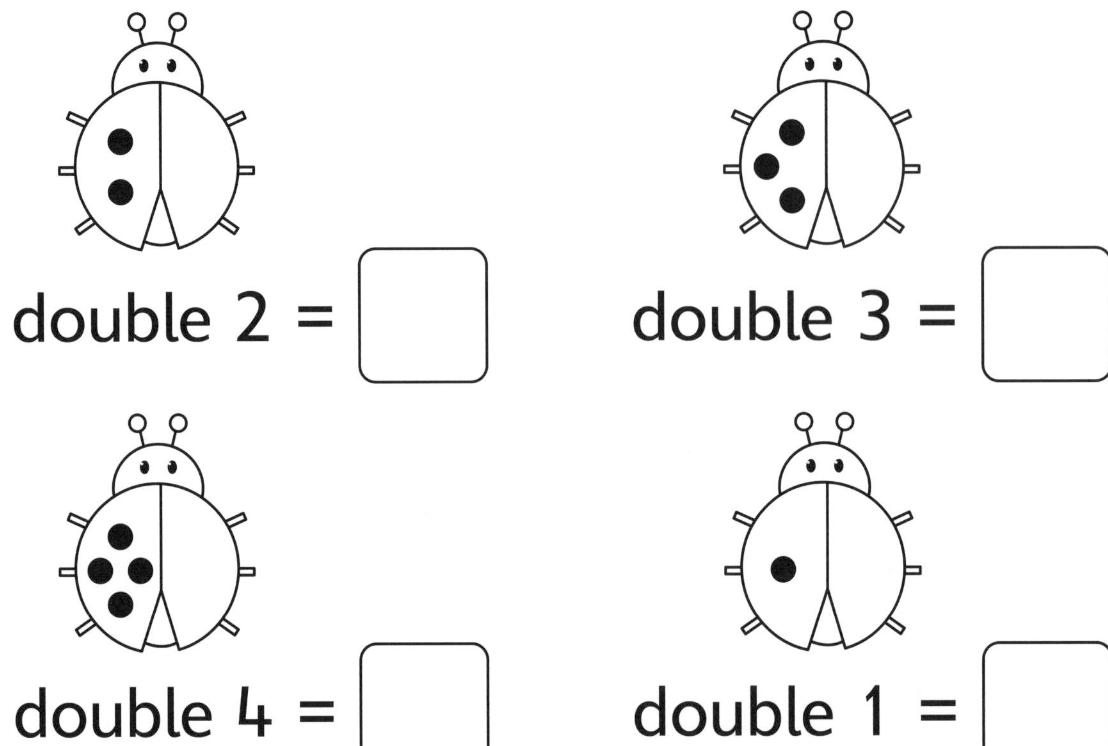

2 **Write** the number statement to match the dice.

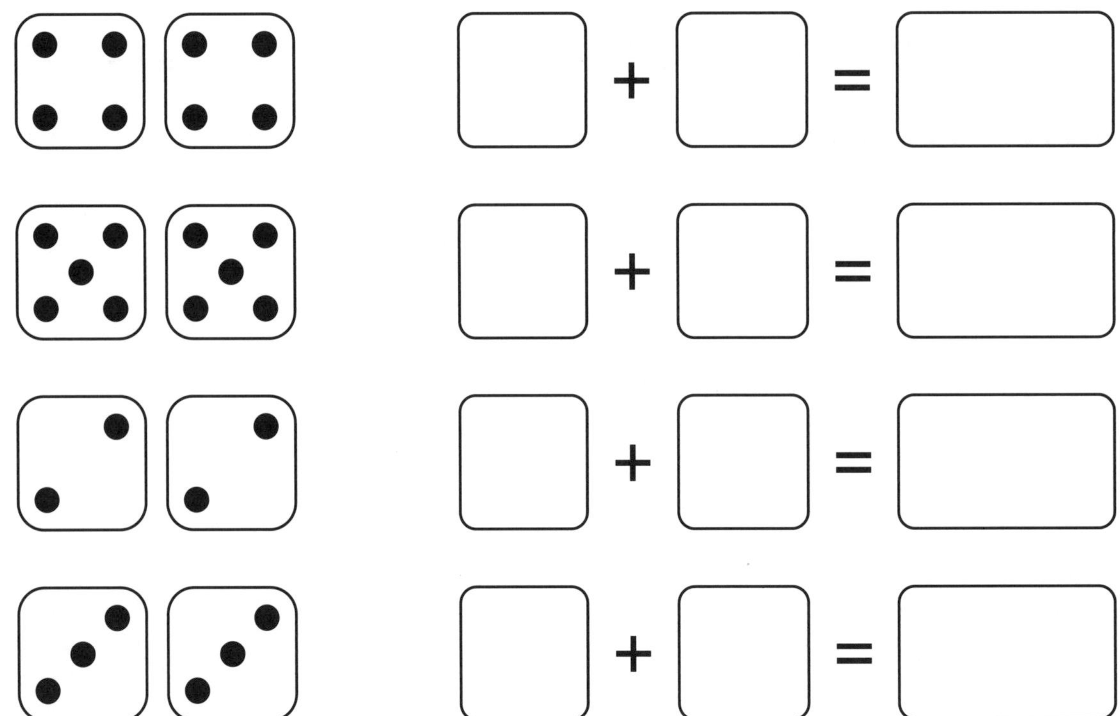

3 **Fill in** the missing numbers using the dominoes.

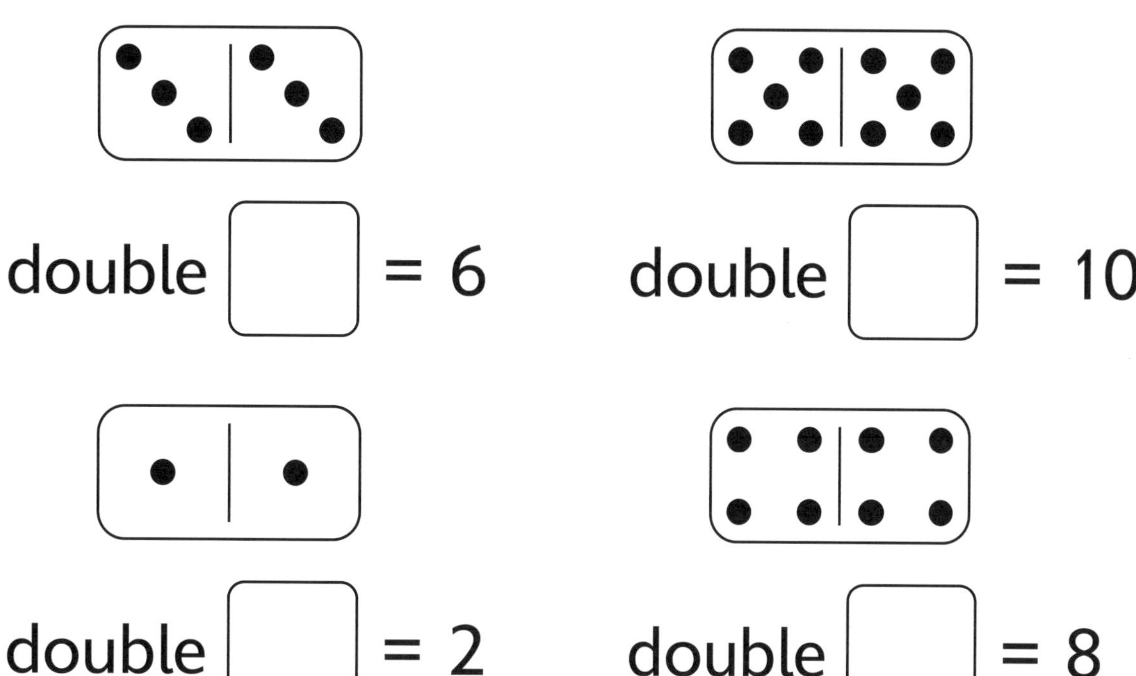

double ☐ = 6

double ☐ = 10

double ☐ = 2

double ☐ = 8

4 Here are the materials needed to make **two** sock puppets.

Write the amount of each material needed to make **four** sock puppets.

= ☐

= ☐

= ☐

= ☐

Sharing into equal groups

1 **Draw lines** to share the fruits equally between the baskets.

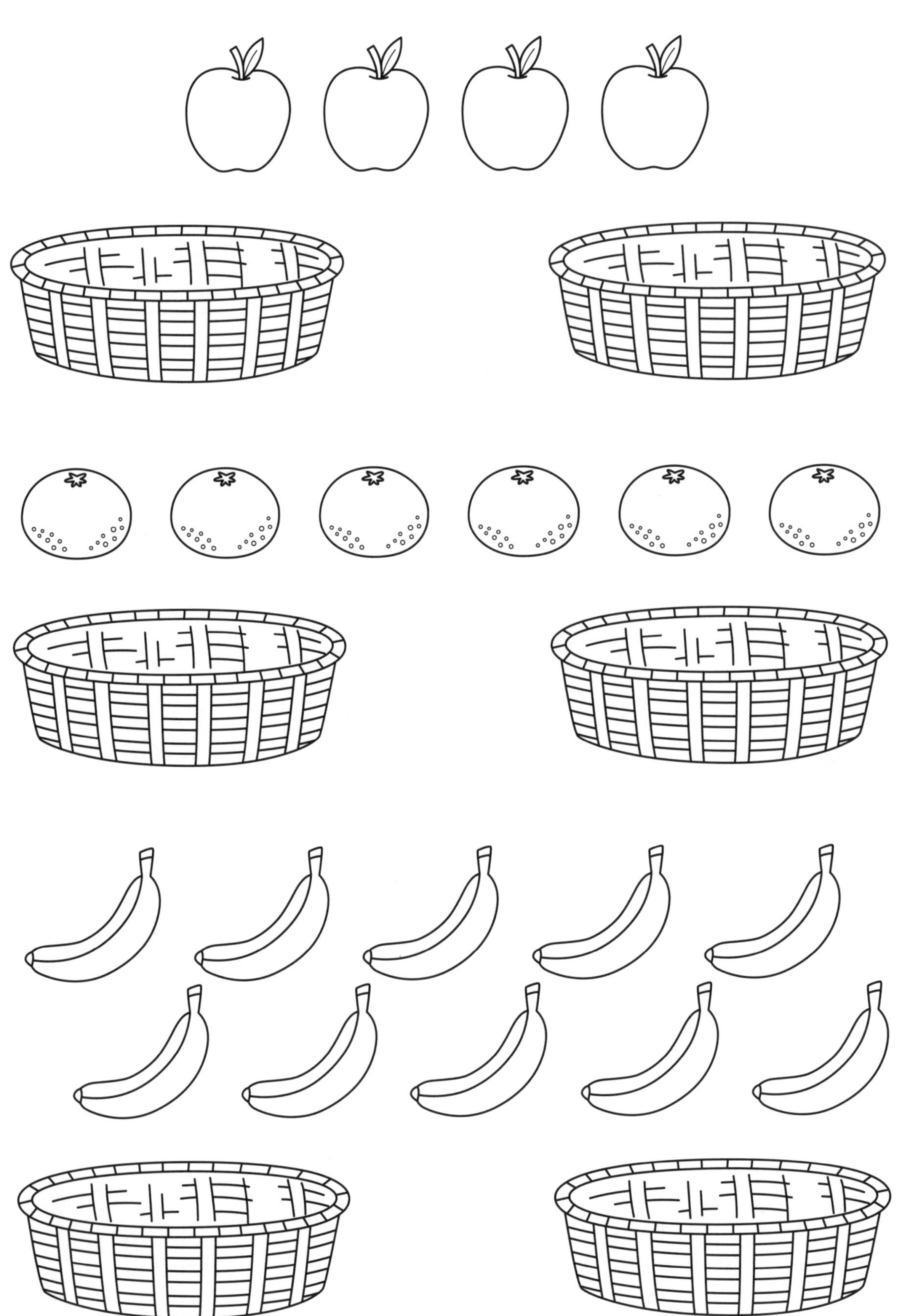

2 **Fill in** the missing numbers in the sentences to match the picture.

☐ berries are shared between ☐ plates.

There are ☐ berries on each plate.

☐ pencils are shared between ☐ pots.

There are ☐ pencils in each pot.

3 **Solve** the number stories.

4 sandwiches are shared equally between 2 bears.
How many sandwiches does each bear get? ☐

2D shapes

(1) **Colour** the first shape. **Trace** the second shape.

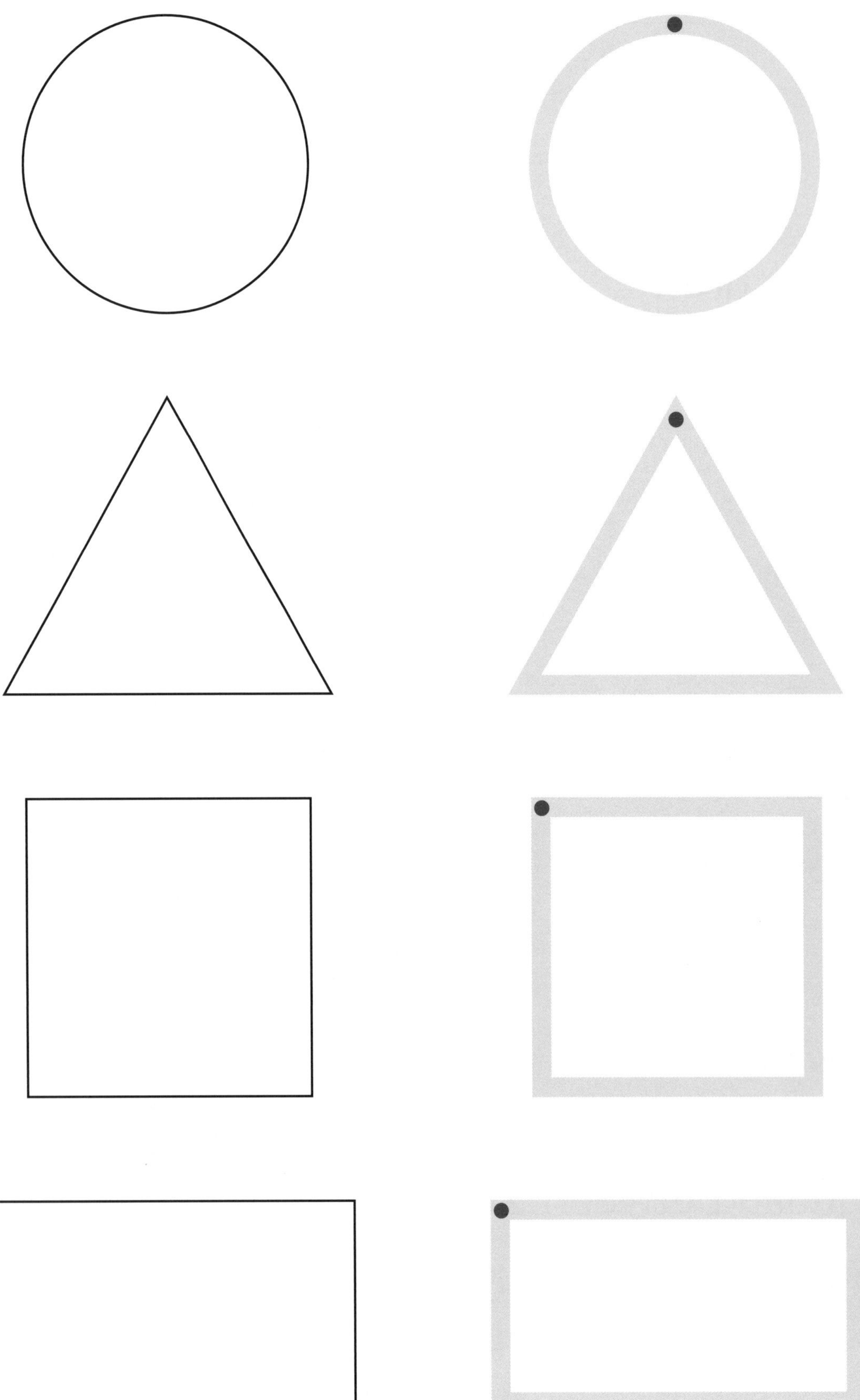

2 **Draw lines** to match each shape to the correct part of the sorting table.

Squares	**Rectangles**

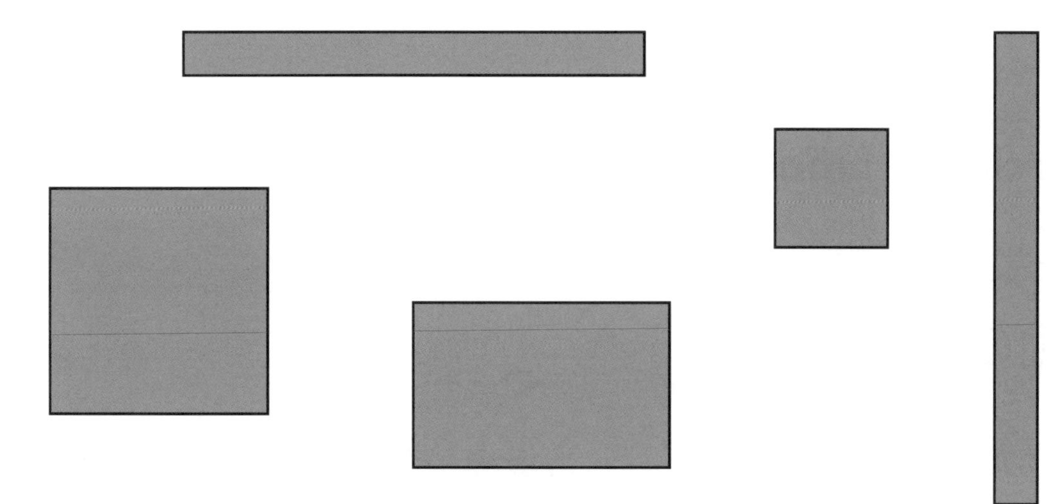

3 **Tick** the shape name of each road sign.

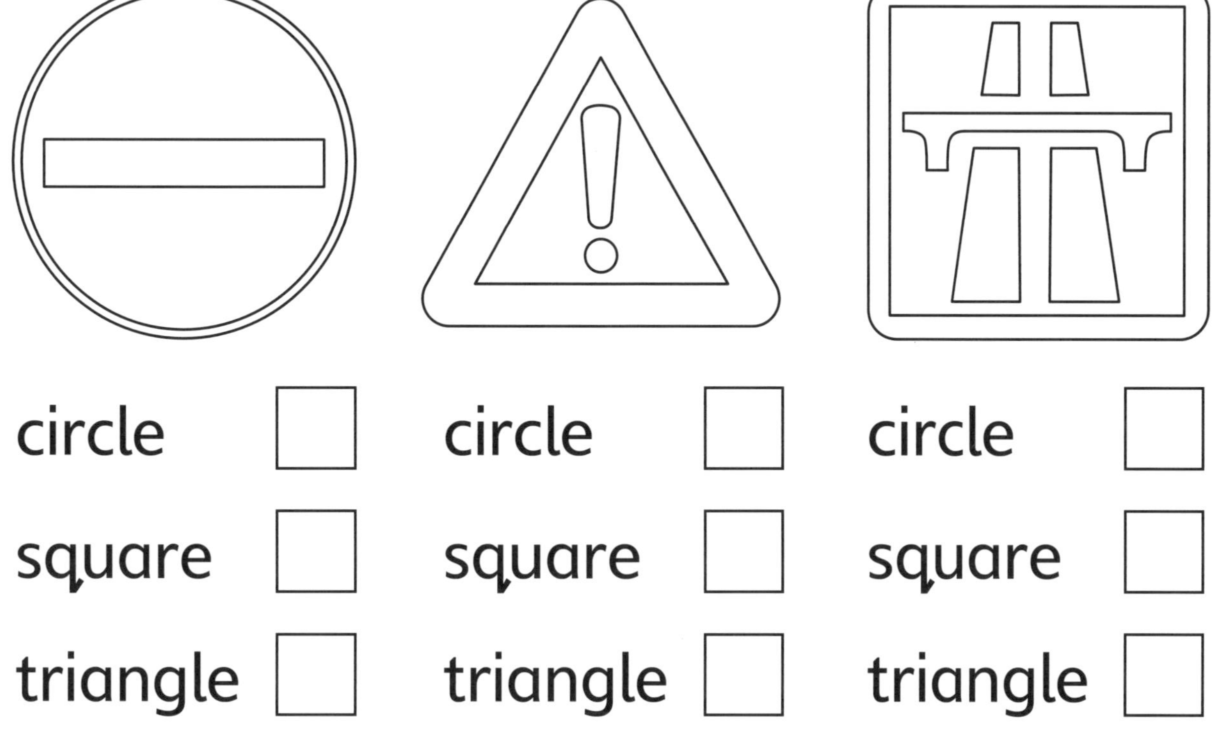

Big and small, long and short

1 **Circle** the **biggest** fruit.

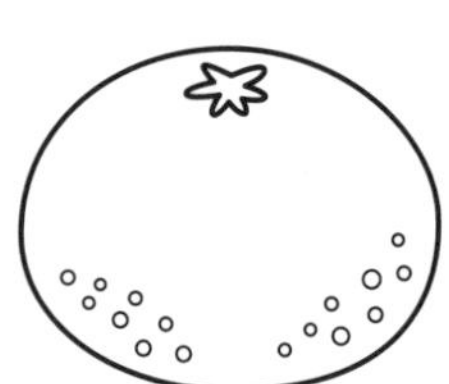

2 **Circle** the **smallest** insect.

3 **Write** the letters of the sea animals in order from smallest to biggest.

A

B

C

__________ __________ __________

smallest biggest

4. **Circle** the **longest** straw.

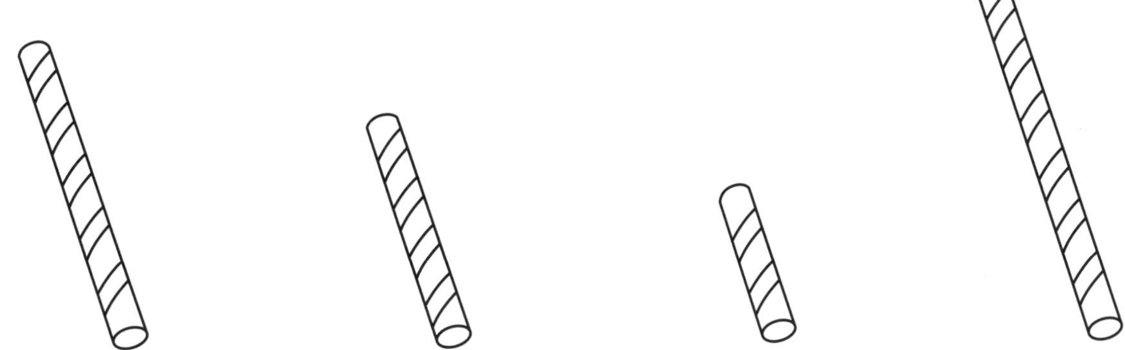

5. **Circle** the **shortest** flower.

6. **Write** the letters of the worms in order from shortest to longest.

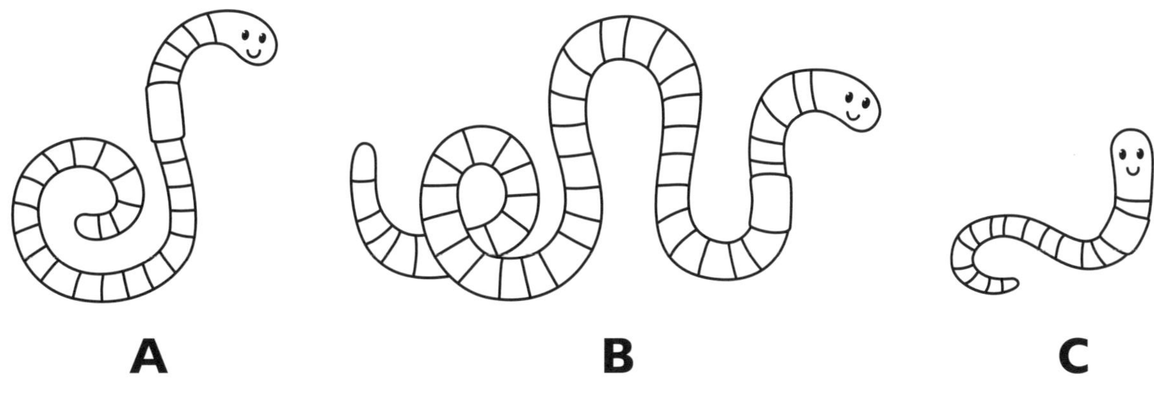

_______________ _______________ _______________

shortest longest

Heavy and light, full and empty

1 **Circle** the **heaviest** animal.

2 **Circle** the **lightest** ball.

3 **Order** the items from heaviest to lightest.

A **B** **C**

__________ __________ __________

heaviest lightest

4 **Circle** the **empty** glass.

5 **Circle** the **fullest** jug.

6 **Order** the bottles from fullest to emptiest.

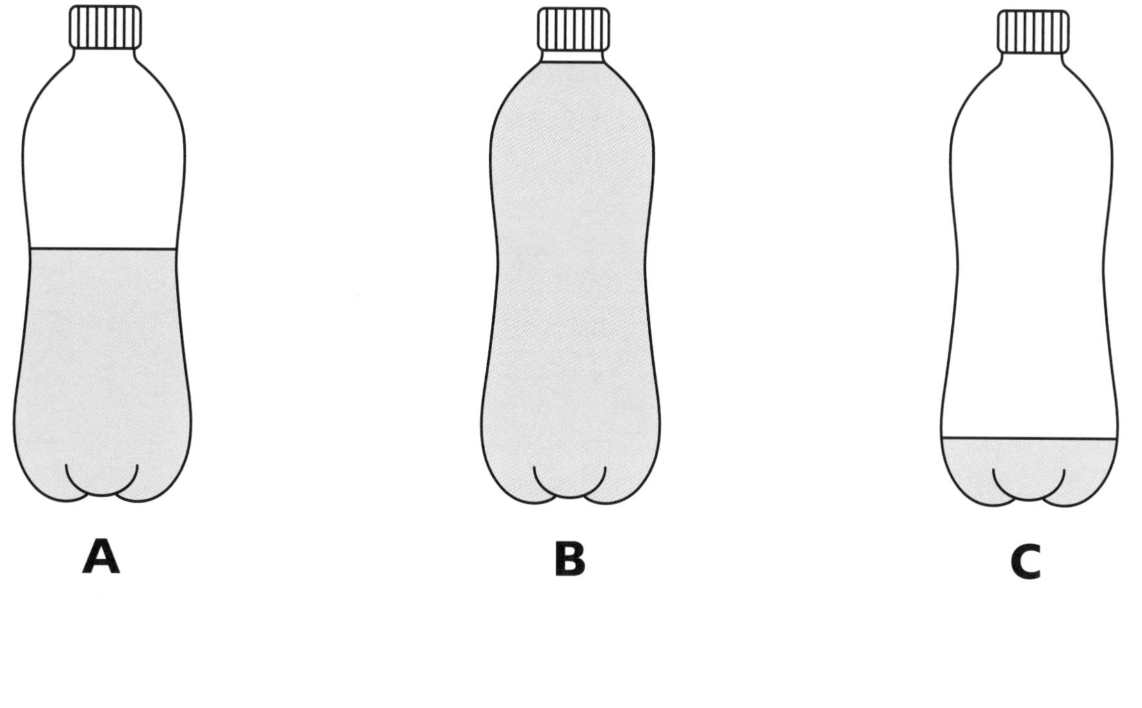

__________ __________ __________

fullest emptiest

Thick and thin, wide and narrow

1 **Circle** the **thickest** sandwich.

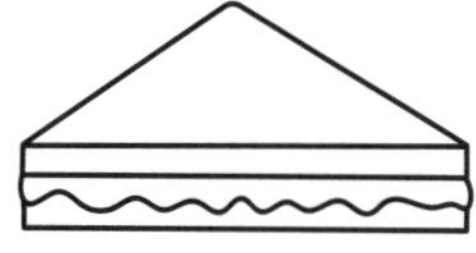

2 **Circle** the **thinnest** book.

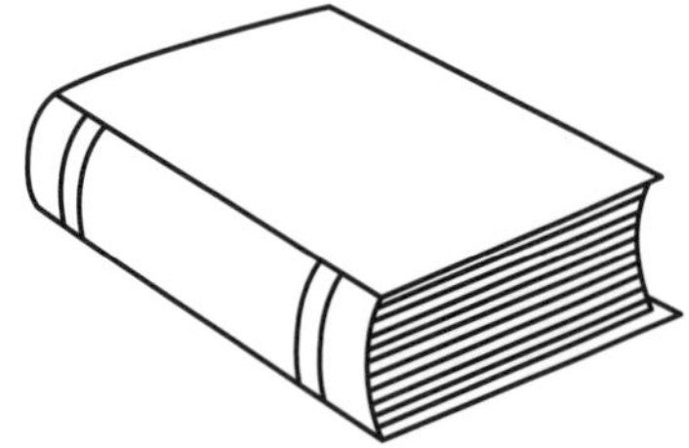
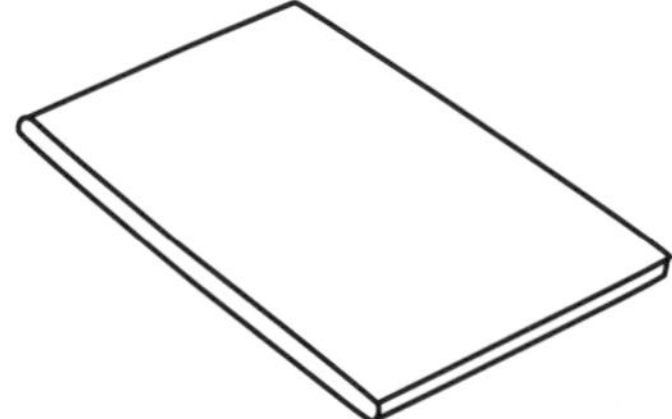

3 **Order** the items from thickest to thinnest.

A

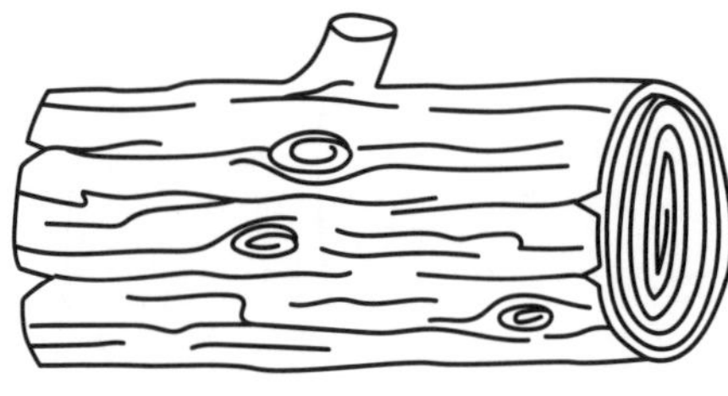

B

C

________ ________ ________

thickest thinnest

(4) **Circle** the **widest** bed.

(5) **Circle** the **narrowest** ribbon.

(6) **Order** the doors from narrowest to widest.

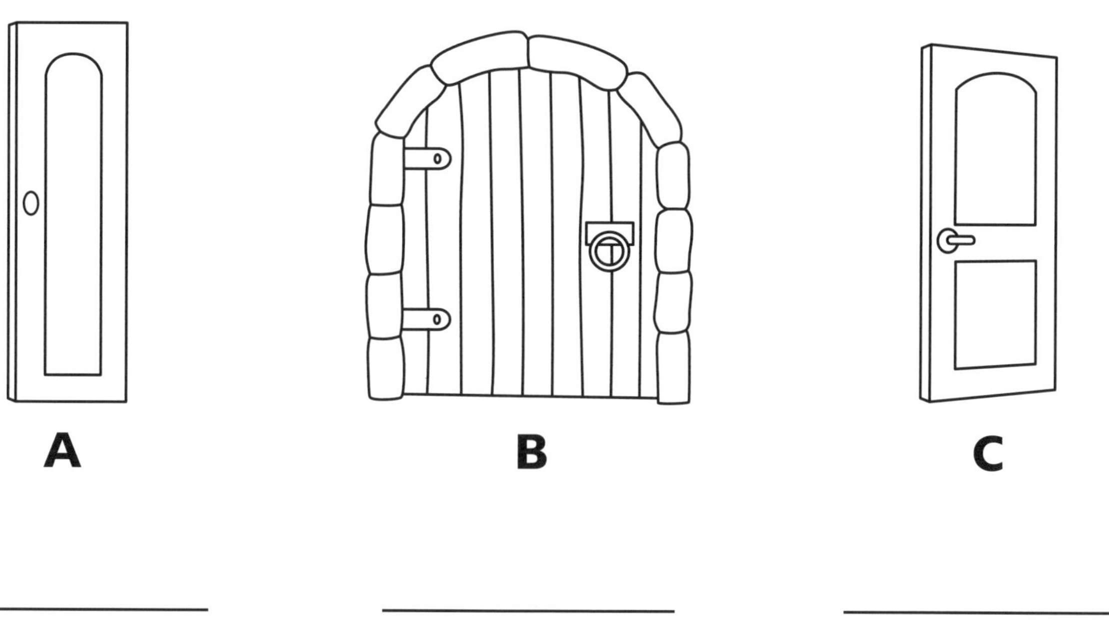

__________ __________ __________

narrowest widest

Coins

1 **Draw lines** to match each coin to how much it is worth.

50p

20p

10p

£1

2p

5p

2 **Draw lines** to sort the coins into the correct purses.

coins **less than** 10p

coins **more than** 10p

3 **Write** how much money this is.

Pattern

1 **Draw lines** to match each pattern to the fruit that comes next.

2 **Draw** the shapes to complete the pattern.

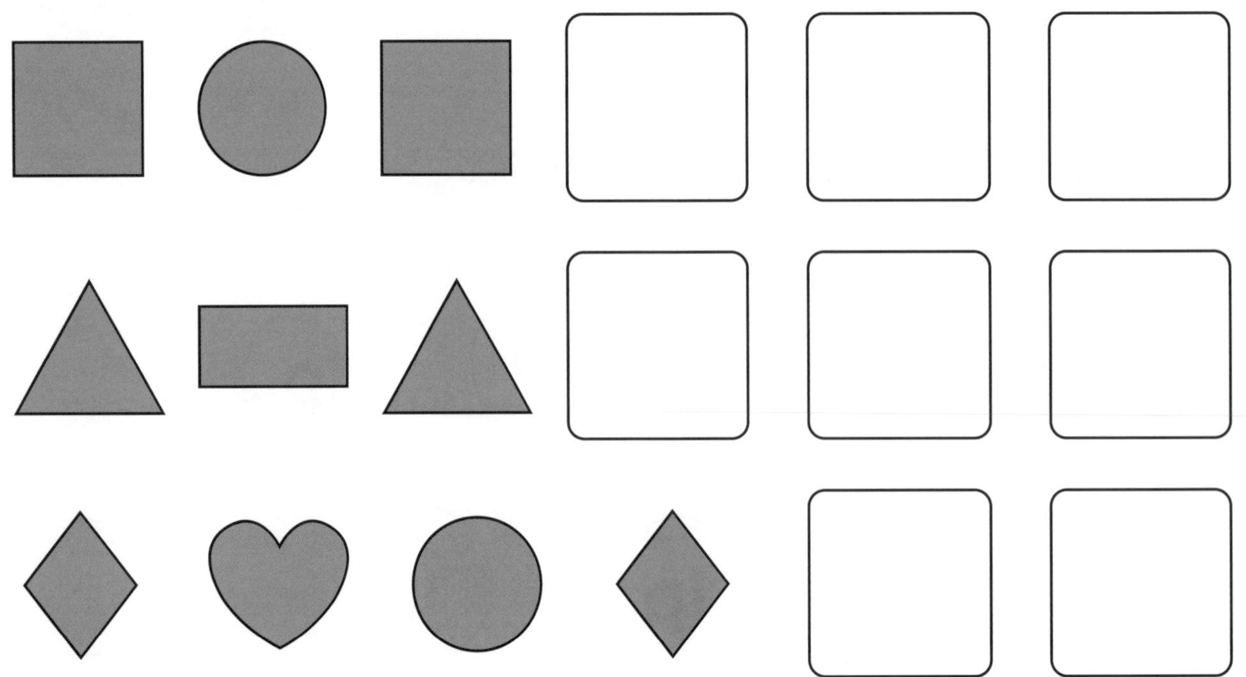

3 **Draw** the missing shape in these patterns.

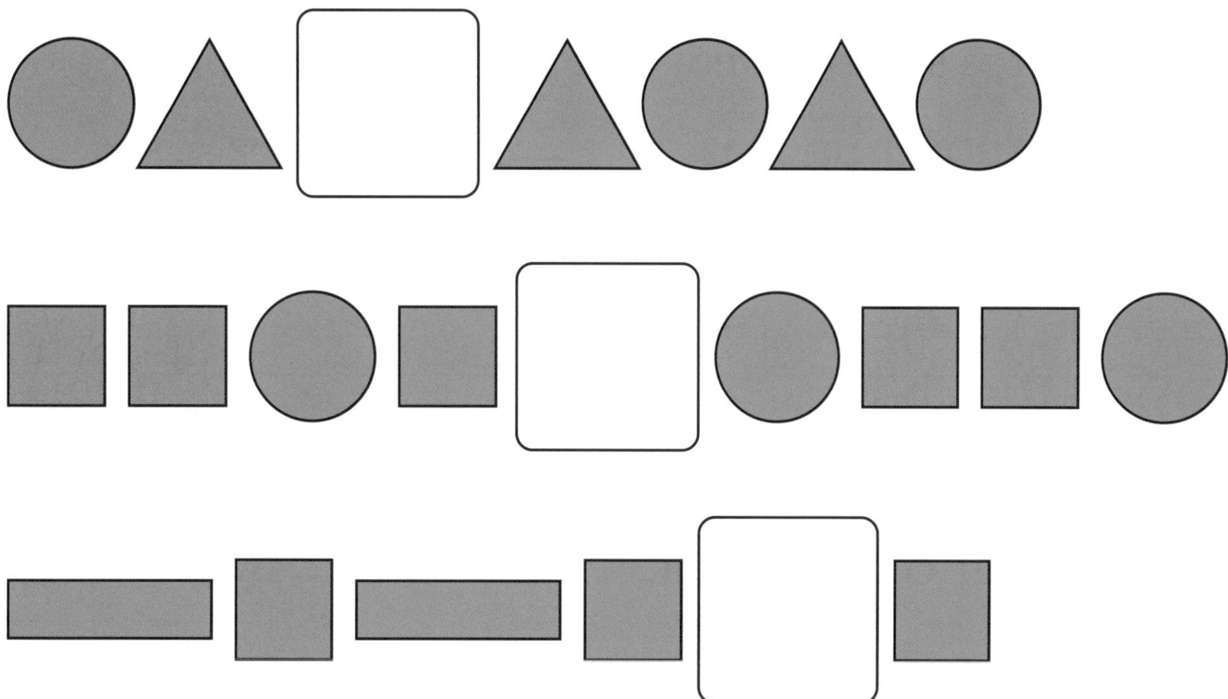

4 **Circle** the ice cream that doesn't fit in the pattern.

5 **Draw** your own pattern.

Position

1. **Tick** the sentence that matches the picture.

The teddy bear is under the chair. ☐

The teddy bear is on the chair. ☐

The teddy bear is in front of the chair. ☐

2. **Tick** the sentence that matches the picture.

The teddy bear is inside the box. ☐

The teddy bear is below the box. ☐

The teddy bear is out of the box. ☐

3. **Tick** the sentence that matches the picture.

The teddy bear is on top of the slide. ☐

The teddy bear is under the slide. ☐

The teddy bear is next to the slide. ☐

4. **Tick** the sentence that matches the picture.

The teddy bear is under the hat. ☐

The teddy bear is next to the hat. ☐

The teddy bear is on the hat. ☐

5. **Tick** the sentence that matches the picture.

The teddy bear is under the ball. ☐

The teddy bear is next to the ball. ☐

The teddy bear is on top of the ball. ☐

6. **Tick** the sentence that matches the picture.

The teddy bear is in front of the trees. ☐

The teddy bear is between the trees. ☐

The teddy bear is under the tree. ☐

Time

1 **Write** the time shown on each clock.

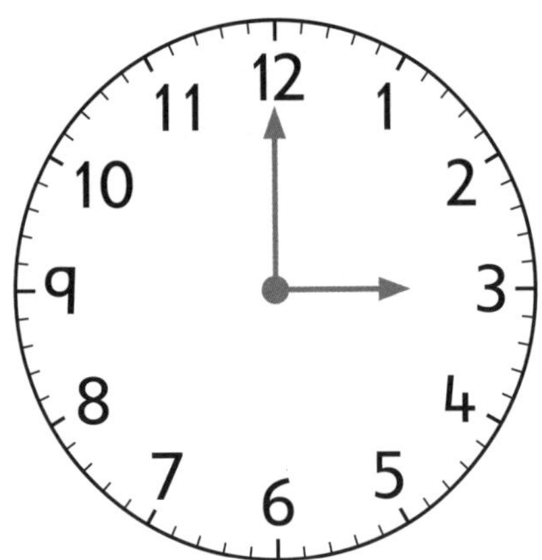

_________ o'clock

_________ o'clock

_________ o'clock

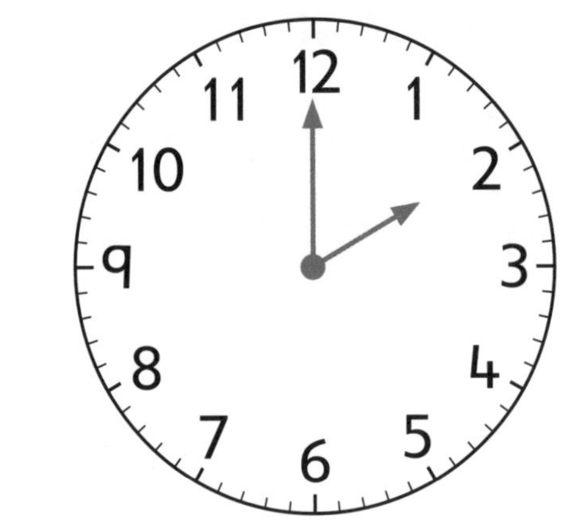

_________ o'clock

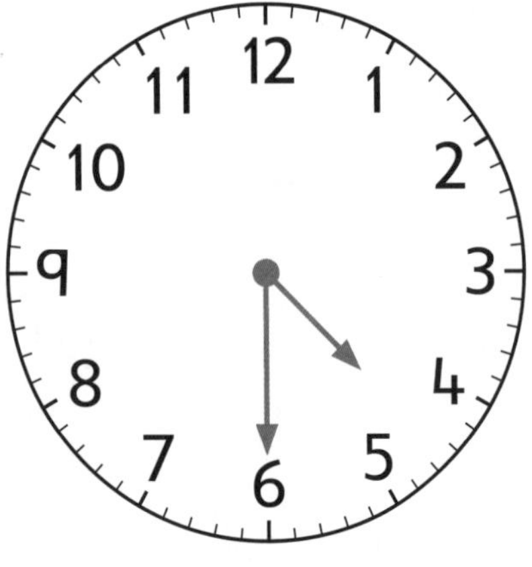

half past _________

half past _________

② **Draw** the correct time on each clock to match the picture.

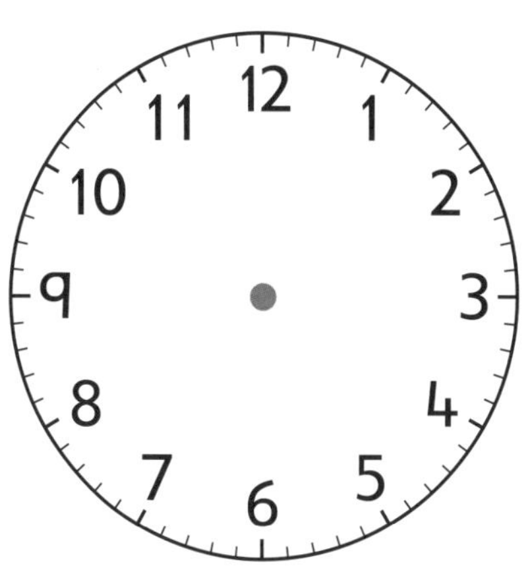

Tom plays football at 10 o'clock.

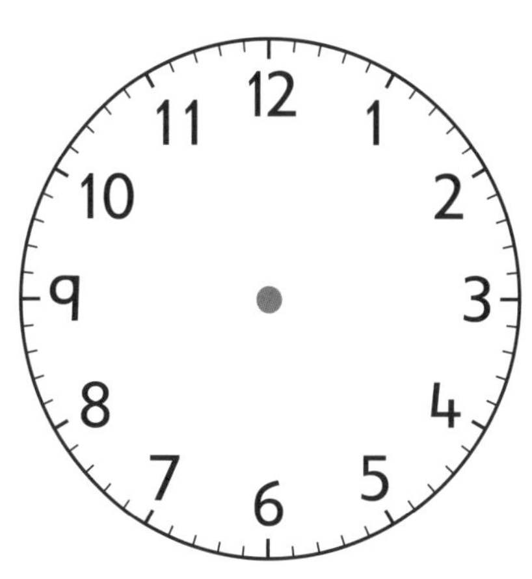

Sara eats lunch at midday.

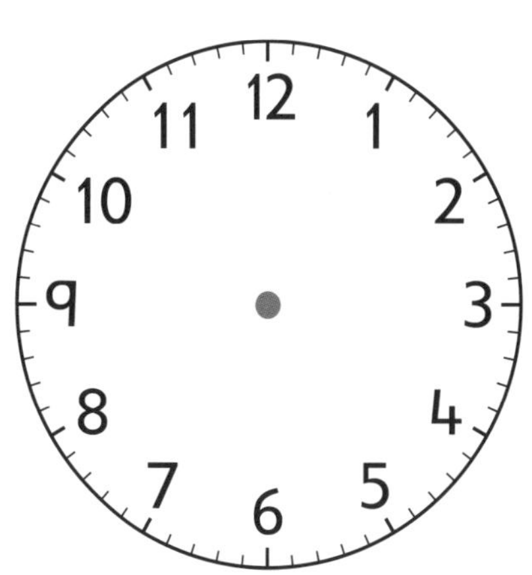

Leo reads at half past four.

Final practice

1 **Count** the objects in the picture. **Write** the numbers.

There are  sandcastles. 

There are  seashells. 

There are  beach balls. 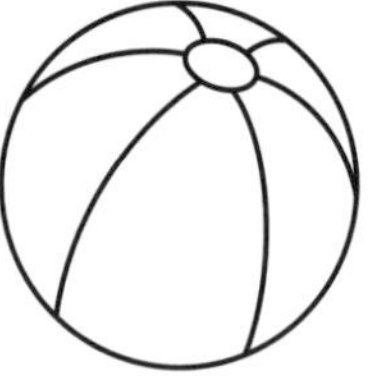

There are  seagulls. 

Final practice

2 **Fill in** the missing numbers on these ladders. Part of one has been done for you.

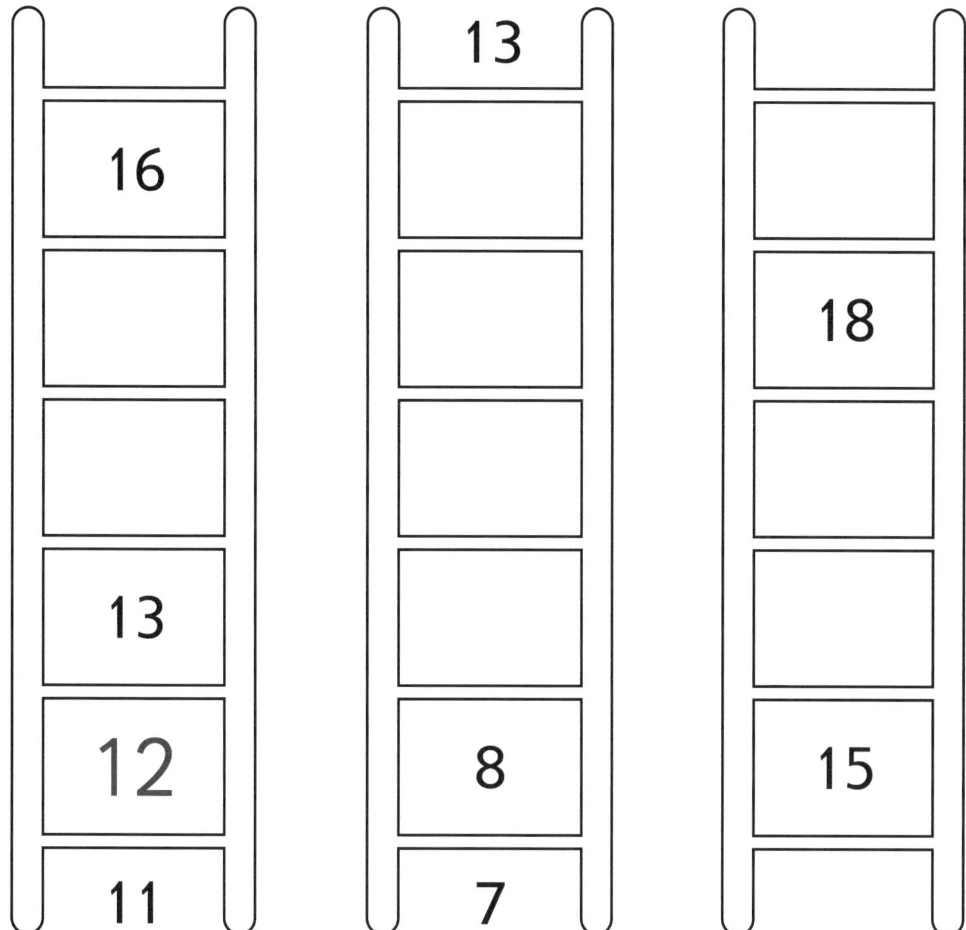

3 **Draw** more flowers to make 10.

Final practice

4 **Write** the numbers to complete the number statements.

★★★ + ★★ = ☐

★★★★★★ − ★★ = ☐

★★★★★ + ★★★ = ☐

★★★★★★★ − ★★★★ = ☐

5 **Draw lines** to match the object to the correct flat shape.

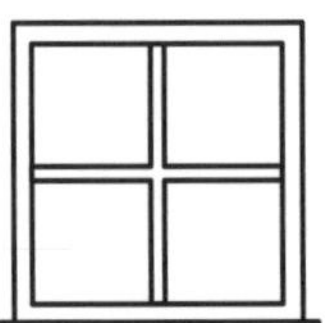